GCSE BITESIZE revision

Check and test

Resistant materials

Design and Technology

Terry Bendall

Published by BBC Educational Publishing,
BBC White City, 201 Wood Lane, London W12 7TS.

First published 2002   Reprinted 2003

© Terry Bendall/BBC Worldwide (Educational Publishing), 2002. All rights reserved.

Illustrations © Oxford designers and illustrators, 2002

Colour reproduction by Spectrum Colour, England

Printed and bound by Poligrafico Dehoniano, Italy

Contents

About GCSE Bitesize

GCSE Bitesize is a revision service designed to help you achieve success in the GCSE exams. There are books, television programmes and a website, which can be found at **www.bbc.co.uk/education/revision**. It's called Bitesize because it breaks revision into bite-sized chunks to make it easier to learn. Check and Test is the latest addition to the Bitesize revision service.

How to use this book

This book is divided into the 100 essential topics you need to know, so your revision is quick and simple. It provides a quick test for each bite-sized chunk so you can check that you know it!

Use this book to check your understanding of GCSE Resistant materials. If you can prove to yourself that you're confident with these key ideas, you'll know that you're on track with your learning.

You can use this book to test yourself:

- during your GCSE course
- at the end of the course during revision.

As you revise, you can use Check and Test in several ways:

- as a summary of the essential information on each of the 100 topics to help you revise those areas
- to check your revision progress: test yourself to see how confident you are with each topic
- to keep track and plan your time: you can aim to check and test a set number of topics each time you revise, knowing how many you need to cover in total and how much time you've got.

GCSE Bitesize revision materials

There's nothing like variety for making revision more interesting, and covering a topic from several different angles is an ideal way to make it stick in your head. There are lots of GCSE Bitesize Revision materials in different media, so take take your choice and make learning enjoyable.

The GCSE Bitesize Revision: Design and Technology website provides even more explanation and practice to help you revise. It can be found at: **www.bbc.co.uk/education/revision**

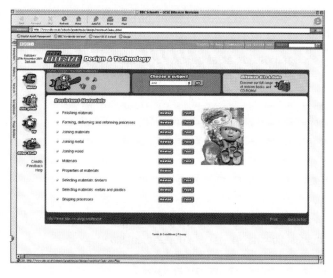

Good luck!

Check the facts

A design brief is a short statement that tells the designer what will be designed and made.

It should include the following things:

- the nature of the product
- who will use the product
- where the product will be used
- where the product will be sold.

A design brief can be open or closed.

An open design brief allows for a wide range of possible ideas to be developed.

A closed design brief is more specific about what is required.

Example of an open design brief

Design and make a lighting unit to provide supplementary lighting in the home. It should be capable of being used in any room in the home and will be sold in specialist lighting shops or in department stores.

Example of a closed design brief

Design and make an adjustable desk lamp to be used when working at a desk or table at home. It should be suitable for a teenager's bedroom. The product will be sold in specialist lighting shops or in department stores.

Test yourself

Write open and closed design briefs for the following situations:

1 a lockable storage device for bicycles used to travel to school

2 storage of collections of small objects.

Designing

www.bbc.co.uk/revision

Check the facts

> A specification is a statement that tells the designer exactly what the product has to do and what the design requirements are.

A specification will always:

- describe what the product has to do
- describe what the product will look like
- include details of any other requirements.

In detail, a specification should include the following information about the product:

- the main function of the product
- the main overall dimensions of the product
- the main materials that are likely to be used
- an outline of the appearance of the product
- special considerations or constraints of the users
- details of the source of power, if needed
- how anthropometrics and ergonomics affect the design
- the cost of the product
- possible production levels – one-off, batch or mass production
- legal requirements that may have to be met
- environmental considerations and requirements.

Test yourself

Write a specification for the following products:

1 a collecting box for a charity that has parts which moves when coins are placed in it

2 a folding chair to be used in schools when exams take place.

Designing

BBG GCSE Check and Test: Resistant materials

Designing

Check the facts

Initial ideas are the possibilities you have thought of for a product, which will meet the requirements of the design brief and specification. For your GCSE coursework project, you should develop at least ten different ideas, but it is useful if you can think of more than ten.

Where do ideas come from?

It is quite difficult to think of totally new ideas for products. You can develop ideas in the following ways:

- Evaluating existing similar products – how well do they do their job? How could they be changed or improved?

- Doing observational and analytical drawings of products – looking at bridges might provide ideas for book storage systems, drawing seed pods of plants could provide ideas for body adornment.

- Thinking about what the product has to do – what are its attributes? This can be developed from the specification.

- Brainstorming – put down in written or sketch form any possible ideas, however unlikely they might be.

Test yourself

Use the suggestions above to produce three possible ideas for the following products:

1 a lockable storage system for use at home for a bicycle

2 a display system for a collection of small objects.

Check the facts

Once you have produced a range of possible ideas for a product, you need to decide on one idea to develop.

How to decide on the idea to choose

When selecting which idea to develop, you need to look at your design brief and specification and make sure that your idea meets them. There are four important things that you need to think about when developing your chosen idea:

- the shape and form of the product
- the materials that could be used
- the way in which the chosen materials can be cut, shaped and joined
- the finish that could be applied.

You need to research all of the possible methods and decide which ones to use. Make sure you give reasons for your decisions in your design folder.

Test yourself

Look at the drawing of the display system below.

1 List the possible materials that could be used to make this product.

2 List the ways in which the materials could be cut to size.

3 List the ways in which the materials could be smoothed ready to start making.

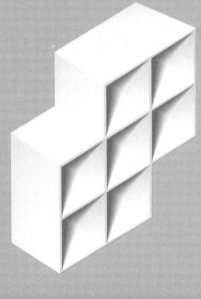

Designing

BBC GCSE Check and Test: Resistant materials

Check the facts

Materials

Models are often used to develop design ideas in industry, schools and colleges. Materials that can be used for making models include card, soft wood (such as balsa), obeche or pine, rigid foam, construction kits, wire and small sizes of metal rod. Welding rod is good for wire frame models.

Types of models

- Models can be solid block models to show ideas. These are good for product design ideas such as mobile phones and torches.

- Models in wood and card are good for furniture.

- Wood and wire are good for models of metal constructions.

- Construction kits are useful to model moving parts. Often, a wide range of materials are combined for models.

Finishes for models

Some models are used to try out ideas quickly and may not need a finish. Models for product design can be painted and made to look very much like the real thing. The type of model and the finish applied will depend on the purpose of the model itself.

Test yourself

Suggest materials for models of the following products:

1 a climbing frame for young children

2 a container for an electronic night light circuit

3 a book storage unit.

Check the facts

Testing can be used to help make decisions about materials and components that could be used to make a product.

Aspects that could be tested and testing methods

The chart below shows some things that could be tested and how the tests might be carried out.

Materials – strength	Identify load the component will have to carry. Apply a load to the material. Measure bending.
Materials – ductility	Use a piece of material of the same size. Try to bend to the required shape. Record the results.
Materials – malleability	Use a piece of material of the same size. Try to form it as required, using the methods specified.
Materials – fusibility	If soldering or welding is required, test on a scrap piece to ensure the process can be done without harming the material.
Materials – working properties	Practise techniques to ensure that materials can be cut and shaped as planned.
Components – power	Test motors to ensure that they have sufficient power output at the correct operating voltage.
Systems – pulleys and gears	Build sample systems, checking sufficient power is transmitted, and friction is reduced to a minimum.

When you carry out tests, record the results in your design folder.

Test yourself

List three tests that could be carried out to identify suitable materials to use for the display system shown in the drawing for topic 4.

Designing

BBC GCSE Check and Test: Resistant materials

Check the facts

If you are not sure which processes to use in making, it is useful to practise techniques. Practising techniques also allows you to decide the degree of accuracy required, and if you are able to achieve it. The degree of accuracy means how closely a component is made to the measurements on a drawing. For example, a woodwork joint should be accurate to about 0.3 mm. The length of the legs of a small table should be accurate to 1.0 mm. Decisions can then be made about which processes to use for making a product.

Aspects that could be tested and testing methods

The chart below shows some things that could be tested, and how the tests might be carried out.

Joining methods	Practice joints can be made. Techniques such as brazing or soldering can be tried out.
Using hand tools	Hand tools that you have not used before can be tried out to develop skills.
Using power tools	Power tool such as routers can be tried out to check that you can control them. (NB teacher supervision needed.)
Using machine tools	Machine tools that you have not used can be tried to check that you can use them effectively and safely. (NB teacher supervision needed.)
Finishing processes	Small samples of the material to be used can have finishes applied. Compare the results.

When you carry out tests, record the results in your design folder.

Test yourself

Decide on the degree of accuracy for the following situations:

1 two steel tubes to be brazed at 90° for a frame

2 a hole to take an aluminium rod 8 mm diameter.

Check the facts

Once an idea has been finalised, you need to plan the order of work for making. Think about the following points:

- the materials that will be needed
- the tools and equipment that will be needed
- the processes that you will need to use
- the components that you will need to buy
- health and safety when making.

All of these points need to be fitted into the time that you have to make the product.

When planning you need to work out the following:

Materials – how long will it take to cut out the component parts and shape them?

Tools and equipment – how long will you need special tools that other people might also want to use?

Processes – how long will it take to do the various jobs? Include time for glue and finishes to dry.

Components – how long will it take to buy special components? Will you have to order them in advance?

Health and safety – what are the possible hazards? How can the risk of harm be reduced?

Test yourself

Produce a time plan for making the wooden box shown in the drawing.

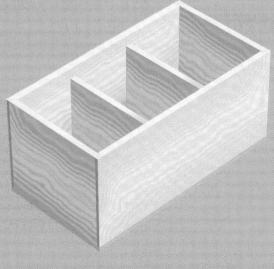

Designing

BBC GCSE Check and Test: Resistant materials

Shaping and finishing materials

Check the facts

Shaping materials by wasting means that material is cut away to leave the desired shape. The material that is removed, such as shavings or sawdust, is usually thrown away, thereby giving the name 'wasting'. Shaping by wasting techniques can be done on any type of material.

Process	Wood	Metal	Plastics
Cutting straight lines	Tenon saw (dovetail saw for fine work)	Hacksaw (junior hacksaw for small work)	Hacksaw (junior hacksaw for small work)
Cutting curved lines	Coping saw (fret saw for fine work)	Abra saw (piercing saw for fine work). Tin snips can be used on thin sheet metal.	Abra saw (piercing saw for fine work). A coping saw can also be used.
Trimming cut edges to a straight line	Jack plane or smoothing plane	Flat or hand file	Flat or hand file
Trimming cut edges to a curved line	Spokeshave or rasp	Round or half round file	Round or half round file
Cutting grooves and slots	Tenon saw to cut sides, then wood chisel or coping saw.	Drill holes at ends, then use abra saw.	Drill holes at ends, then use abra saw or piercing saw.

Test yourself

Name the tools used for the processes shown in the drawings.

1 Cutting the slot in pine 50 mm wide and 20 mm thick.

2 Cutting the shape out of 1 mm thick copper sheet.

3 Smoothing the rough corner on 6 mm thick acrylic.

Shaping and finishing materials

Check the facts

The machines listed below can be used to shape materials using wasting techniques. For health and safety reasons, some of these processes may have to be done for you by your teacher.

Process	Wood	Metal	Plastics
Cutting curved lines	Jig saw, either fixed or portable, with suitable blade. A band saw can be used by a teacher to do this task.	Bench mounted jig saw (with suitable blade). A band saw can be used by a teacher to do this task.	Jig saw, either fixed or portable, with suitable blade. A band saw can be used by a teacher to do this task.
Making holes	Drilling machine and suitable drill bits	Drilling machine and twist drills	Drilling machine and twist drills
Creating round shapes of different diameters	Wood turning lathe	Metal turning lathe	Metal turning lathe
Cutting grooves and slots	Hand router or CNC milling machine	Vertical milling machine or CNC milling machine	Vertical milling machine or CNC milling machine

A Computer Numerically Controlled (CNC) milling machine has the advantages of accuracy and being able to repeat the task many times.

Test yourself

Name the machines used for the processes shown in the drawings.

1 Cutting this shape by machine from 10 mm thick MDF.

2 Cutting a slot 15 mm wide in 10 mm thick aluminium alloy.

3 Drilling four 10 mm diameter holes in 6 mm thick acrylic.

BBC GCSE Check and Test: Resistant Materials

Check the facts

Deforming is a method of shaping materials by bending either in a straight line or by creating a bowl or dish shape.

Methods of deforming in two dimensions are outlined below. Bending can be done on metal or thermoplastics.

- Thin metal may be bent cold in a vice or in folding bars. A mallet is used to prevent damage if soft metal is being bent.

- Larger pieces of metal may need to be made hot before bending. Softening the metal by annealing may be required.

- Thermoplatiscs are bent using a strip heater or line bender that will heat the plastic in a straight line.

- Wood is bent by laminating (see topic 59). This can be done in a mould or by the use of a vacuum bag press.

Test yourself

Draw a picture of wood being laminated in a mould.

Shaping and finishing materials

www.bbc.co.uk/revision

Check the facts

> Deforming in three dimensions cannot be done on wood.
> Plastics materials must be heated in order to deform in 3D.

Hollowing is normally done on thin sheet metal. The metal should be annealed first. A leather sand bag, or hollowed wooden block is used with a bossing mallet.

Vacuum forming is used to shape plastics material to a bowl shape. A wooden mould has to be made first. The plastic is heated and shaped by creating a vacuum under the sheet. Air pressure forces the plastic over the mould.

Blow moulding is used to shape plastics – mainly for making bottles and similar shapes such as plastic buckets. The plastic is put into a mould and air pressure blows the plastic to the sides, creating the desired shape.

Press moulding can be used on metals and plastics materials. A mould is made in two halves – top and bottom. The sheet material is placed between the two halves and pressure applied. For metal, a bench vice or fly press is used. For plastics, the sheet must first be heated in an oven before putting it into the mould. Pressure can be applied by hand or in a vice.

Test yourself

1 Name two examples of products made by vacuum forming.

2 Sketch the process of press moulding.

Shaping and finishing materials

BBC GCSE Check and Test: Resistant Materials

Fabrication techniques

Check the facts

Fabrication involves joining separate pieces of material by cutting joints or by using other components, such as screws and nails or adhesives, or by using heat processes, such as soldering or welding.

Fabrication processes can be temporary or permanent, depending on whether they can be taken apart easily or not.

The chart below gives an outline of fabrication techniques and when they might be used.

Process	Wood	Metal	Plastics
Joints – permanent	Wide range of different joints, used in conjunction with suitable adhesives.	Usually only simple butt joints used, joined by welding or soldering.	Usually only simple butt joints used, joined by glues or heat gun.
Nails, pins – permanent	Nails used for some work where appearance is not so important. Panel pins useful for fixing thin plywood and MDF.	Not used	Not used
Threaded fastenings – temporary	Wood screws of various types used.	Machine screws, self-tapping screws and nuts and bolts.	Machine screws, self-tapping screws and nuts and bolts.
Heat processes – permanent	Not used	Soldering, brazing and welding used on most metals.	Some plastics can be welded using a heat gun that melts the plastic together.
Rivets – permanent	Not used	A useful way of joining. Pop rivets mainly used.	Rivets can be used to join plastics, but not usually.
Adhesives – permanent	Usually used with wood joints, but not always.	Some limited use, more in industry than in schools.	Plastics often joined with adhesives that melt and fuse the material.

Test yourself

1 Describe the difference between permanent and temporary joining methods.

2 Give an example of permanent and temporary joining methods for wood, metal and plastics.

Check the facts

> Reforming is a method of shaping materials
> by changing their overall appearance, by melting
> or softening into a paste form.

Reforming methods of shaping material include casting, injection moulding and extrusion.

Casting

Most metals can be cast but school casting normally uses aluminium. When casting in metal, the required shape is made in a soft material, usually wood. This is called a **pattern**. A mould is made in special casting sand inside a moulding box or flask. The sand is made to stick together using water or oil. The pattern is removed and metal poured into the cavity.

Die casting uses a metal mould and can include very fine detail. Die casting is a very important industrial process used for many different types of products. The mould is made in two parts to allow the casting to be removed.

Injection moulding

Injection moulding is a similar process to die casting. A metal mould is used and softened plastic, in a paste form, is forced into it by pressure from a screw thread or pneumatic cylinder. The mould is made in two parts to allow the moulding to be removed. Injection moulding is used extensively in industry.

Extrusion

Extrusion is used to produce long but fairly thin products. Examples of extruded products include curtain tracks and the frames for replacement windows. Both plastics and metal can be extruded. The material is forced through a die, which contains a hole that is the same shape as the required product.

Test yourself

List two examples of products made by sand casting.

Shaping and finishing materials

BBC GCSE Check and Test: Resistant Materials

19

Shaping and finishing materials

Check the facts

All products are made up of a number of different components. Often these will need fine adjustment so that they fit together correctly and with a neat finish. Fitting the parts may involve some of the following processes:

Joints in wood may need small amounts of waste wood removed so that they push together easily. For a well-fitting joint it should be possible to push the joint together and for it to stay together when turned upside down. Careful chiseling of the wood is much better than filing or sanding. The two surfaces that touch should not have gaps.

The sides of wooden and metal frames should be parallel and have 90° corners, unless planned otherwise. When assembled, three-dimensional frames should also be parallel. Check with try squares and by measuring the diagonals of the frame.

Sawn surfaces need to be smooth and flat. The end grain of wood should be sanded and edges planed smooth and sanded if needed. Metal and plastics should be filed and draw-filed smooth. Final cleaning up of all materials should be done with suitable abrasive paper. Polish may be needed on some plastics and metals.

Test yourself

List two checks that should be made before assembling a wooden stool.

Check the facts

A finish is the term used to describe a coating or process carried out when the product has been assembled and all marks and scratches left from the making have been removed.

When applying a finish, you need to make sure that it is safe for the use to which the product will be put. Items in contact with food, for example, may be left in their natural condition. The chart below describes a range of finishes for wood, metal and plastics.

Type of finish	Material used on	Description
Varnish	Wood	Usually applied using a brush. Allows the wood grain to be seen. May be used for interior and exterior work. Some varnishes can be used to give a coloured appearance.
Paint	Wood, metal	Usually applied using a brush. Is opaque so surface underneath cannot be seen. Used for interior and exterior work. Several coats may be needed.
Wood preservatives	Wood – exterior products	Usually applied using a brush. Allows the wood grain to be seen. Used on garden furniture and wooden buildings. May have a coloured effect.
Wax polish	Wood	Usually applied to products used indoors. Allows the wood grain to be seen. Gives a high shine.
French polish	Wood	Usually applied to products used indoors. Allows the wood grain to be seen. Gives a high shine, but needs many coats to do so.
Enamel	Metal	Applied to copper to give a decorative effect.
Plastic coating	Metal	Thin coating of plastic applied to hot metal, forming a protective layer of plastic over the surface of the metal. Used on outdoor furniture and toys.
Polishing	Metal, plastics	The metal is polished by hand or with the aid of a buffing machine to give a high shine. Normally used on interior products.
Oil blacking	Mild steel	The metal is heated to a low temperature and cooled in oil. This leaves a dark blue surface finish.
Lacquer	Metal	Used on polished metal to prevent tarnishing.

Test yourself

Give suitable finishes for the following products:
1 a tool box made from mild steel
2 a garden seat made of pine,
3 a copper dish.

Using ICT

Information and Communications Technology (ICT) can be used to help with designing in the following ways:

- Written information of any type can be written using word processing software.
- Writing and drawings can be combined using desktop publishing (DTP) software.
- Drawings can be produced using drawing or design software.
- Pictures of existing products which you find can be scanned and used in DTP work.
- Pictures of products which you find on the Internet can be saved and included in DTP work.
- A database can be used to record survey information.
- Graphs and charts can be used to record your survey information in a graphical form.
- Text can be re-sized and shaped using DTP or graphics software and printed out for a range of uses.

ICT can be used when making in the following ways:

- Shapes printed onto card can be used for templates.
- Text printed out can be glued onto sheet material and cut out.
- Machines for cutting card and self-adhesive vinyl sheet can be used to cut letters or shapes. Complicated shapes can be cut more easily than by hand.
- Computer controlled milling machines cut out shapes more easily than cutting by hand, especially recesses in materials.
- Computer controlled lathes can be used to make a number of identical parts.

Test yourself

State an ICT process which could be used for the following tasks:

1 recording the results of a survey

2 producing a time plan

3 cutting a wooden letter shape and a recess which it will fit into accurately.

Check the facts

These terms are used mainly in industry, but may be used in schools as well.

Terms used to describe ICT in industry

CAD – Computer Aided Design

CAM – Computer Aided Manufacturing

CIM – Computer Integrated Manufacturing

FMS – Flexible Manufacturing Systems

CNC – Computer Numerical Control

PDM – Product Data Management

CADMAT – Computer Aided Design, Manufacturing and Testing.

Although ICT is normally used in mass production, it is also useful in one-off or small batch work.

Complicated shapes are produced more easily than by hand. In small batch production, control sequences can be changed to produce different products.

Reasons why ICT is used in industry

- Data can be stored electronically and retrieved easily.
- Designs can be modelled on-screen and viewed from any angle.
- Reaction to outside forces, such as wind flow and pressure, can be modelled.
- Designs can be altered quickly.
- Zoom facilities allow for the whole product, or details, to be seen easily.
- Libraries of standard components can be stored electronically and integrated into new designs.
- Control sequences for making can be simulated before working on the actual material.
- CNC manufacturing is normally more accurate.

Test yourself

Suggest three products made by industrial methods where ICT could be used to assist in the making.

Using ICT

BBC GCSE Check and Test: Resistant Materials

Using ICT methods for modelling is an important part of designing in industry.

Two-dimensional modelling is done using CAD software to draw out components and see how they fit together. **Three-dimensional modelling** can also be done using CAD software to produce 3D drawings.

It is now possible to produce virtual reality models of products on a computer that not only show the finished product, but can show it in a suitable environment and under different conditions, such as different lighting conditions. Another type of 3D modelling will show how parts move on the product, and if one part will hit another when moving.

Why use ICT-based modelling in industry?

- A design can be modified easily.

- Outline ideas can be illustrated quickly.

- Designs can be modelled on-screen and viewed from any angle.

- The way in which parts move can be shown, and any clashes between parts seen.

- Designs can be transmitted electronically to other locations.

Test yourself

Give three reasons why modelling using ICT methods is more effective than making 3D models by hand.

Check the facts

Terms used to describe production methods in industry:

- **One-off** – only one of a product is made.

- **Batch** – a small quantity of the product is made: two or more, up to about 100.

- **Mass production** – a large number of the product is made, usually on a production line. Sometimes this is called **repetitive flow production**. Many hundreds of the product can be made.

- **Continuous flow** – many thousands of the product are made. The difference between this and mass production is that the production line is kept running 24 hours a day, seven days a week.

One-off production is labour intensive as every product is different. Batch production may also be labour intensive but jigs and templates are used to aid production. Batches of the product can be made as often as required. Often the machines can be easily changed to produce a batch of a different product.

Repetitive flow often involves the assembly of a number of sub-assemblies of individual components. **Continuous flow** is used where the process is automated and few workers are required. It is also used where it would be expensive to start and stop the production process.

Test yourself

Give two examples of products that could be made using each of the production methods described.

Check the facts

Terms used to describe commercial manufacturing systems:

- **Cell production** – a group of machines and/or work places where a single component or sub-assembly is produced.
- **In-line assembly** – an assembly line where a product is put together from sub-assemblies and other components.
- **Just-in-time** – materials, components and sub-assemblies are delivered to the place where the product is made and assembled just in time for production.
- **Logistics** – the process of planning to ensure that all materials, components and the finished products are delivered when needed.

Test yourself

Look at the picture of the electric fan. It consists of a number of parts. These are:

base, switch control assembly, cover and main support, joining piece to connect the motor housing to the main post, motor cover, electric motor, linkage to allow fan to rotate, fan blade, two-part fan guard.

List those parts that could be common to the following fans and might be bought in assemblies:

1 a wall fan

2 a floor-standing fan.

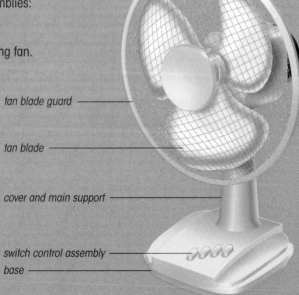

fan blade guard ⎯⎯⎯⎯⎯

fan blade ⎯⎯⎯⎯⎯

cover and main support ⎯⎯⎯⎯⎯

switch control assembly ⎯⎯⎯⎯⎯

base ⎯⎯⎯⎯⎯

Industrial applications

www.bbc.co.uk/revision

Check the facts

- **Packaging** – the box or other container that holds the product and protects it during transport and while it is in the shop.
- **Marketing** – this involves understanding who the product is for and the sort of products they want.
- **Advertising** – is about planning how to tell people about a new or improved product.

The package for any product needs to include information about the product:

- what it is made from
- where it was made
- the name of the manufacturer
- operating instructions
- any safety information needed
- how the product should be stored, both in the shop and when bought.

To ensure effective marketing, **market research** is used to find out what people want from a product. Market research can be carried out by questionnaires, surveys, interviews, test selling and information about other similar products available for people to buy.

Advertising is done through:

- advertisements in newspapers and magazines
- hoardings
- radio and television
- the Internet
- direct mail shots.

Usually several methods will be used for the same product. The aim is to bring the product to the attention of as many people as possible.

Test yourself

1 List three ways in which the product could be advertised.

Check the facts

In industry, quality is about:

- meeting the specification
- ensuring that the product does what it is supposed to do
- making sure that there are no defects in the product
- making sure that all the products are right first time, every time
- making sure that customers are satisfied with the product.

> **Quality planning is about planning ways to make quality criteria and check that they are met.**

> **Quality control is about checking the product at all stages of production.**

Testing for quality

Quality needs to be tested at all stages of making a product. Before testing for quality, you must decide what the quality checks need to be, and when the work will be checked.

You can test for quality in the following ways:

- **Check measurements** – are they within the tolerances specified?
- **Check the fit of joints** – are they fitted accurately and neatly without gaps? Are soldered and welded joints finished neatly?
- **Check for appearance** – are surfaces smooth and free of dents and scratches? Are the proportions of the product appropriate?
- **Check for working** – do parts move as required? Does the product work as intended?
- **Check against the specification** – does the product meet all aspects of the specification?

In your GCSE project, the tests that you carry out for quality control can be used as the basis of your evaluation.

Test yourself

List the quality control tests that could be applied to the display unit shown in the drawing.

Check the facts

Charts help to plan the use of your time or to plan the making of a product. There are several different types of planning charts that can be used.

- **Flow charts** describe in words the sequence of operations.
- **Sequence diagrams** show the process of making in words and pictures.
- **Gantt charts** show the tasks involved in making a product and if there can be overlaps in different tasks.

> When making a **flow chart**, remember that 'starts and 'finish' boxes are round-ended boxes, 'processes' are put in rectangular boxes and 'decisions' are in diamond-shaped boxes. Flow charts are useful for fairly simple tasks.

> **Sequence diagrams** show how a task is done, using pictures and notes. They are useful if you need to tell someone else how to do a job or how to use something.

> **Gantt charts** are useful for complex planning where various tasks can be done at the same time, or where two or more people are working on the same product.

Test yourself

Draw a sequence diagram for making a mortise and tenon joint.

Planning and evaluation

Check the facts

There are two sorts of product evaluation:

- evaluation of existing products
- evaluation of products that you design and make.

Existing products can be evaluated using several different methods.

Using the product

The product is used and the following questions answered:

- Is it easy or convenient to use?
- Does the product do its job?
- Does it appeal to the user?

Performance testing

The product is tested to see that it meets its specification and the following questions asked:

- Does it do the job for which it was designed?
- Does it fit into the place where it is used?
- Does it meet other specification requirements?

Testing if the product is appropriate

A check is made to see if a product meets the needs of the users and the environment. The following checks can be made.

- Does it suit the needs of the users?
- Are the materials used transported over long distances?
- Is it made in the local area?
- Are the energy sources and the materials used renewable?
- Is the use of the product, and its disposal after use, friendly to the environment?

Test yourself

Use one of the methods described above to evaluate the following products:

1 a mobile telephone

2 a bicycle

3 a wooden kitchen stool.

Check the facts

A finished product can be evaluated to see that:

- it meets the design need or situation
- it meets the needs of the intended users
- it is fit for the purpose for which it is intended.

When evaluating a product to check that it meets the needs listed above, you can do some of the following things.

Design needs

Look back at your notes to see what the need or situation was. Check to make sure that your product meets this need. For example, if you made a rack to store CDs, can you get the CDs in and out easily?

User needs

Check that the person who is going to use the product likes the final product. Does it fit into their home? Is the cost appropriate?

Fitness for purpose

Does the product do what was intended? For example, if you make an adjustable lamp, is it stable? Does it direct the light where it is needed?

Test yourself

Look at a product that you have designed and made in the past. Did it meet the needs as described above? List any points that were not met.

Check the facts

Values in Design and Technology cover the following areas:

- **Technical values** – concerned with aspects such as accuracy, reliability, benefits of machine processes over hand processes, use of bought-in components, degree of finish required, and so on.

- **Moral values** – concerned with aspects such as use of sustainable resources, cost of products, images used in a product. Do they cause offence, is the product desirable or needed?

- **Cultural values** – concerned with aspects such as lifestyle, fashion, influences of the design of products from other times and other cultures, having the same products as others in your social group, and so on.

- **Environmental values** – concerned with the use and sources of materials, the use of energy and the disposal of waste materials. Also concerned with pollution and environmental harm caused during making.

How to evaluate a product for value considerations

Values will vary according to the nature of the product. Firstly, decide what values will be involved in the product that you are designing and making. This should be done at the specification stage. Once you know what the values are, you can check to see how well your product conforms to the value issues you have identified.

Test yourself

List the value issues involved in the design of the following products:

1 a coffee table made from a tropical hardwood timber

2 jewellery

3 a storage rack made mainly from plastics materials.

Check the facts

Appropriate use of materials involves the following aspects:

- Using the most appropriate materials for the components of the product – for example, checking that the properties of the material are suitable for the intended purpose. Would a veneered panel be more appropriate than the use of a solid piece of timber?

- Making sure that material is used economically. For example, when cutting parts from sheet material, or standard lengths of material, make sure that parts are set out to make the best use of the size of sheet or length.

- Making sure that any finish is appropriate for the type of material and the use to which the product will be put. For example, a timber with a decorative grain would not normally be painted. Some finishes are not suitable when used on products to be used with food.

Test yourself

Look carefully at your last piece of practical work and the design folder for it. Check the use of materials. List any aspects of designing and making where more appropriate use could have been made of materials.

Check the facts

Appropriate use of resources involves the following:

- Using machines appropriately and with care. Machines can often do a job more quickly and accurately than by hand. The amount of material cut off in one go should not strain the machine or damage it.

- Use jigs and templates to make making quicker and more accurate where a process has to be done several times.

- Where the same process has to be done on several components, get all the pieces ready for that process. This saves setting up machines a second time.

Often it will be necessary to check by research and testing that resources have been used appropriately. In your design folder, include details of how this research was done.

Test yourself

Look carefully at your last piece of practical work and the design folder for it. Check the use of resources. List any aspects of designing and making where more appropriate use could have been made of resources.

Check the facts

An important part of evaluating is to check that the product does what it is supposed to do and, where necessary, to suggest or make modifications to make it work better. Sometimes this will involve testing and evaluating making processes, including jigs and templates, and changing these to give a better product.

Examples

If you were making a CD rack, such as that shown in diagram 1, which needed a number of curved metal rods to hold the CDs, it would be better to make a jig so that they were all the same. A design for a possible jig is shown in diagram 2.

Diagram 1
CD rack

hole to locate metal

Diagram 2
Bending jig

The jig needs to:

- allow for the metal to be bent to the required amount
- allow the metal rod to be put in easily and taken out easily after bending
- ensure that all the rods are bent to the same angle.

You need to make about five rods to check that the jig worked correctly and alter it if necessary. You also need to make sure that you used the same material for the tests as for the production run. If you used a different type of metal, the results could be different.

Test yourself

State two things that would need to be tested before this jig is used to make a batch of the component.

Check the facts

When jigs have been evaluated, it may be necessary to modify them in order to make sure that they do the task correctly.

Example

If, when the product was finished, you found that the CDs were not held correctly because the rods are not at the correct angle, you need to correct the fault. This could be done by adding a piece of wood to the base as shown in diagram 1. It would, however, have been better if a jig had been made to ensure that the rods were at the correct angle, and for this to be tested before making the actual rack.

Diagram 1
Side view of CD rack to show extra
piece of wood used to increase angle

Test yourself

Diagram 2 shows a jig that could be used for drilling the holes for the rods. Describe how this could be altered to increase the angle at which the holes are drilled.

Diagram 2
Drilling jig for holes

peg locates in
previous hole

Side view showing
jig in use

Check the facts

The main materials for Design and Technology are wood, metal and plastics, but other materials are used on some occasions.

The main classification of materials is given in the chart below. You need to know these terms.

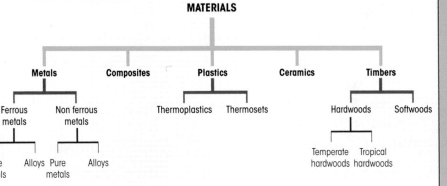

MATERIALS

- Metals
  - Ferrous metals
    - ...als
    - Alloys
  - Non ferrous metals
    - Pure metals
    - Alloys
- Composites
- Plastics
  - Thermoplastics
  - Thermosets
- Ceramics
- Timbers
  - Hardwoods
    - Temperate hardwoods
    - Tropical hardwoods
  - Softwoods

Basic information about material classifications

- Ferrous metals contain iron. Non-ferrous metal do not contain iron.

- Alloys are a mixture of two or more metals or elements such as carbon.

- Thermoplastics can be heated and shaped many times. Thermoset plastics can only be heated and shaped once.

- Hardwood timbers are so named because of their cellular structure when seen under a microscope, not because they are hard to cut.

- Composite materials are formed by combining and bonding two or more materials – a reinforcing material and a bonding agent, such as a glue. This is different from an alloy. Sometimes material, such as medium density fibreboard and glass reinforced plastic, are termed composite materials.

Test yourself

1 Name two ferrous and two non-ferrous metals.

2 Name two hardwood timbers.

3 Name two theromoplastics.

Materials and components

Check the facts

The main working properties of materials describe how a material functions when it is being shaped. The main terms used are listed below, although not all terms will apply to all materials.

Fusibility – the ability of a material to change into a liquid or molten state when heated to its melting point.

Conductivity – the ability of a material to conduct heat or electrical energy.

Strength – the ability of a material to withstand a force without breaking or bending.

Elasticity – the ability of a material to bend and then to return to its original shape and size.

Plasticity – the ability of a material to be permanently changed in shape.

Malleability – the ability of a material to be permanently deformed in all directions without cracking.

Ductility – the ability of a material to deform, usually by stretching along its length.

Hardness – the ability of a material to resist wear, scratching and indentation.

Toughness – the ability of a material to withstand blows or sudden shocks without breaking.

Durability – the ability of a material to withstand wear, especially as a result of weathering.

Test yourself

1 Name a ductile metal.

2 Name a tough timber.

3 Name a durable plastics material.

Check the facts

The chart below lists some of the common ferrous metals, their properties and some main uses.

Name and melting point	Composition	Properties and characteristics	Principle uses
Cast iron 1200° C	Iron + 3% carbon	Hard skin softer underneath but brittle.	Parts with complex shapes which can be made by casting.
Mild steel 1600° C	Alloy of iron and 0.15 – 0.35% carbon	Tough, ductile and malleable. Good tensile strength, poor resistance to corrosion.	General purpose engineering material.
Medium carbon steel 1600° C	Alloy of iron and 0.4 – 0.7% carbon	Strong and hard but less ductile than mild steel.	Springs, any application where resistance to wear is needed.
High carbon steel 1800° C	Alloy of iron and 0.8 – 1.5% carbon	Harder than mild steel. Can be heat treated to make harder and tougher.	Cutting tools, ball bearings
Stainless steel	Alloy of iron and carbon with 18% chromium, 8% nickel, 8% magnesium	Hard and tough, resists wear and corrosion.	Cutlery, kitchen equipment
High speed steel	Alloy of iron and 0.4 – 0.7% carbon with tungsten, chromium and vanadium	Very hard, resists heat when used as cutting tool.	Cutting tools for machines

Note: a form of high carbon steel is available, which has a smooth polished finish. It is known as 'silver steel' but the composition is the same as high carbon steel. It does not contain silver.

Test yourself

1 Name a ferrous alloy.

2 Give the composition of stainless steel.

Check the facts

The chart below lists some common non-ferrous metals, their properties and their main uses.

Name and melting point	Composition	Properties and characteristics	Principle uses
Aluminium 660° C	Pure metal	Good strength to weight ratio, light, soft, ductile, good conductor of heat and electricity.	Kitchen equipment, window frames, general cast components
Duralinium	Aluminium with 4% copper, 1% manganese and some magnesium	Strong but lightweight, will harden over time, good machining properties.	Many applications where strength and lightness are required
Copper 1080° C	Pure metal	Malleable and ductile, good conductor of heat and electricity, resistant to corrosion.	Water pipes, electrical wire, decorative goods
Zinc 420° C	Pure metal	Weak metal, extremely resistant to corrosion, low melting point, good for casting.	Usually used for coating steel to make galvanised items, die cast products
Brass 900–1000° C	Alloy of copper and 35% zinc	Resistant to corrosion, fairly hard, good for casting, good conductor of heat and electricity.	Cast items such as water taps and ornaments
Gilding metal	Alloy of copper and 15% zinc	Fairly strong, malleable and ductile when soft.	Decorative goods, architectural fittings
Tin 230° C	Pure metal	Soft, weak, malleable and ductile, resistant to corrosion.	Usually used for coating steel to form tinplate, soft solder

Test yourself

1 Name a non-ferrous alloy.

2 Give the composition of duralimin.

Materials and components

www.bbc.co.uk/revision

Check the facts

The chart below lists some of the common hardwood timbers, their properties and some main uses.

Name and source	Colour	Properties and characteristics	Principle uses
Ash Europe and N. America	Light creamy brown	Open grain, tough and flexible	Tool handles, sports equipment, wooden ladders
Beech Europe and N. America	White to pinkish brown	Close grained, hard, tough and strong	Some furniture, especially chairs, toys
Birch Europe and N. America	Creamy white	Fairly soft and easy to work, open grain	Main timber used for plywood
Cherry N. America	Red brown	Fairly close grain, easy to work	Good quality furniture
Elm Europe and N. America	Light to medium brown	Open and sometimes interlocking grain, tough and durable	Indoor and outdoor furniture
Iroko W. Africa	Yellow brown	Strong, fairly hard, durable, open grain	Garden furniture, science benches
Mahogony C. and S. America, W. Africa	Pink to red brown	Fairly strong, durable	Good quality furniture
Meranti S.E. Asia	Red brown	Fairly strong and durable	Interior joinery, used for making plywood
Oak Europe, Japan, N. America	Light brown	Very strong, hard and tough, will corrode steel screws and fittings	Good quality furniture and interior woodwork
Obeche W. Africa	Pale yellow	Soft, light, not very durable, straight open grain	Some parts of furniture, core plywood
Sapele W. Africa	Red brown	Hard and closed grained	Good quality furniture
Teak India and S.E. Asia	Golden brown	Hard, very strong and durable, very resistant to acids and moisture	High quality indoor and outdoor furniture, science benches

Test yourself

1 Name a timber suitable for making science benches.
2 Name a timber that will corrode steel screws.

Materials and components

Check the facts

The chart below lists some common softwood timbers, their properties and some main uses.

Name	Colour and sources	Properties and characteristics	Principle uses
Parana pine	Pale yellow with red streaks. S. America	Hard, fairly strong and durable, straight grain	Good quality interior woodwork
Scots pine	Pale creamy white. Northern Europe	Fairly strong, easy to work straight grain with some knots	Standard timber for internal woodwork and DIY work
Spruce	Pale creamy white. Northern Europe	Fairly strong, easy to work with some small knots. Can contain resin pockets	Standard timber for internal woodwork and DIY work

Test yourself

1 Name a timber suitable for standard interior work.

2 Describe the properties of Parana pine.

www.bbc.co.uk/revision

Check the facts

The chart below lists some common thermoplastics, their properties and some main uses.

Name	Properties and characteristics	Principle uses
Acrylonitrile butadienestyrene (ABS)	Strong, tough, hard, light, durable, good surface finish, resists chemicals	Casings for kitchen equipment (e.g. food processors), toys, telephones, car components, tool handles.
Cellulose acetate	Tough, hard, stiff, light in weight, transparent, non-flammable	Cases for pens, small tool handles, spectacle frames, small door knobs.
Polyamide (nylon)	Creamy colour, tough, fairly hard, resists wear, self lubricating, good resistance to chemicals, machines well	Bearings, gear wheels, casings for power tools, curtain rail fittings, hinges and catches for small cupboards.
Polymethyl methacrylate (acrylic)	Stiff, hard but scratches easily, durable, brittle in small sections, good electrical insulator, machines and polishes well	Signs of all types, covers of storage boxes, aircraft canopies and windows, covers for car lights, wash basins and baths.
Polypropylene	Light, hard but can scratch easily, tough, good resistance to chemicals, resists 'work fatigue' qualities	Medical equipment, laboratory equipment, containers, especially with built-in hinges, 'plastic' chair seats, string, rope, kitchen equipment
Polystyrene Conventional	Conventional - light, hard, stiff transparent, brittle, good water resistance.	Toys, especially model kits, packaging, cases for televisions, 'plastic' boxes and containers.
Toughened	Better impact strength	Toys, linings for refrigerators.
Expanded	Good compression strength, brittle in tension, lightweight, good heat/sound insulation	Packaging, insulation
Polythene Low density	Tough, good resistance to chemicals, flexible, fairly soft, good electrical insulator.	Packaging, especially bottles, toys, packaging film and bags.
High density	Hard, stiff, able to be sterilised	'Plastic' bottles, tubing, household equipment.
Polyvinyl chloride (uPVC)	Stiff, hard, tough, lightweight, good chemical resistance	Pipes, guttering, bottles, window frames
Plasticised (PVC)	Soft, flexible, good electrical insulator	Covering for electrical cables, hosepipes

Test yourself

1 Name a plastics material suitable for making the handle of a small screwdriver.

2 Describe the properties of low density polythene.

Materials and components

Check the facts

The chart below lists some common thermosetting plastics, their properties and some main uses.

Name	Properties and characteristics	Principle uses
Epoxy resin	Good electrical insulator, hard, brittle unless reinforced, resists chemicals well	Casting and encapsulation, adhesives, bonding of other materials
Melamine formaldehyde	Stiff, hard, strong, resists some chemicals and stains	Laminates for work surfaces, electrical insulation, tableware
Polyester resin	Stiff, hard, brittle unless laminated, good electrical insulator, resists chemicals well	Casting and encapsulation, bonding of other materials
Urea formaldehyde	Stiff, hard, strong, brittle, good electrical insulator	Electrical fittings, handles and control knobs

Test yourself

1 Name a plastics material suitable for making electrical fittings.

2 Describe the properties of melamine formaldehyde.

Check the facts

**Market forms of materials are the shapes
and sizes that the material comes in before
it is cut, shaped and joined.**

Wood

Softwood timber comes in a range of standard cross-section sizes.
Some common sizes are:
25 x 25 mm, 25 x 50 mm, 25 x 75 mm, 25 x 100 mm, 50 x 50 mm,
50 x 75 mm.

It is important to remember that the sizes are those when the wood is
in its rough sawn state. Normally, softwood is bought planed smooth.
This is called **planed all round (PAR)**. Planed wood is smaller than
the sizes given, e.g. 25 x 50 mm is usually about 20 x 45 mm. This is
called the **finished size**. In DIY shops, the finished size is often given.

Hardwood timber can be obtained in similar sizes to softwood
timber. Usually it is possible to get wider boards than softwood.
Hardwood timber is also usually sold by sawn size.

Sheet materials, such as plywood and MDF, are sold in sheets which
are 2440 mm long and 1220 mm wide. Thicknesses of sheet material
range from 1.5 mm to 50 mm. Not all of the common sheet materials
are available in all these thicknesses.

Test yourself

List some common sizes for softwood timber.

Materials and components

BBC GCSE Check and Test: Resistant Materials

Check the facts

Metals and plastics are available in a wide range of sizes and cross-section shapes, although not all shapes are available in all of the sizes.

Metal

Metal is available in bars of standard shapes, e.g. solid round, square, flat, hexagonal and angle section and round and square tube. Sizes of round and square bars range from 1.5 mm to 150 mm. The length of these bars is usually about 3 metres. Flat strips or bars range from 2 mm thick and 6 mm wide, up to 25 mm thick and 300 mm wide.

Metal can be bought in sheets that are 2440 mm long and 1220 mm wide. Thicknesses of sheet material usually range from 1.5 mm to 10 mm.

Plastics

Plastics are also available in lengths of standard shapes, e.g. round, square, flat, angle section and round and square tube. Sizes of round and square bars range from 1.5 mm to 100 mm. The length of these bars is usually about 3 metres.

Plastics can also be bought in sheets that are up to 2440 mm long and 1220 mm wide. Thicknesses of sheet material range from 0.5 mm to 20 mm.

Test yourself

List 10 sizes and types of metal available in your school or college.

Materials and components

Check the facts

Components in Design and Technology are defined as:

Threaded fastenings: wood screws
machine screws
nuts and bolts
self-tapping screws

Rivets: hammered
pop

Hinges, catches and locks

Knockdown fittings

Wood screws are used to join metal or plastics components to wood, or to join two pieces of wood to make a strong joint. See topic 57.

Machine screws have a screw thread to fit into a threaded hole or a hexagonal nut. They can be used to join two or more pieces of metal or plastics.

Bolts also have a screw thread to fit into a threaded hole or a hexagonal nut and are normally used to join two or more pieces of metal or plastics.

Hammered rivets are used to join metal, but are sometimes used on products such as kitchen knives, where a wooden or plastics handle may be riveted to the blade.

Pop rivets were originally designed for use in the aircraft industry but are now used in many different products. See topic 45.

Hinges, catches and **locks** are used on boxes, cabinets and cupboards. There is a wide range of types of all three categories and they can be used on products made from wood, metal and plastics.

Knockdown (KD) fittings are used where something has to be taken apart often, or which is designed for assembly by the user. They are normally plastic fittings that can be joined with one screw or bolt. See topic 57.

Test yourself

1 List two uses for wood screws.

2 Name one way of joining plastics materials to metal.

Materials and components

BBC GCSE Check and Test: Resistant Materials

Check the facts

Marking out needs to be done before cutting. You need to measure from a base line or datum surface.

Creating a datum surface

On wood – use a plane.

On metal and plastics – use a flat or hand file.

Use a steel rule or straight edge to check that a surface is flat. Use a try square to check that a surface is at right angles to another surface.

Marking out tools

Process	Wood	Metal	Plastics
Lines	Pencil	Scriber	Felt tip pen
Lines at right angles to an edge	Carpenters' try square	Engineers' try square	Engineers' try square
Lines parallel to an edge	Marking gauge	Odd-leg calipers	Odd-leg calipers
Marking for a mortise	Mortise gauge		
Marking a circle	Pair of compasses	Dividers	Dividers
Marking the centre of a hole	Pencil	Centre punch	Felt tip pen
Marking an irregular shape	Template	Template	Template

Test yourself

Name the tools used for the processes shown in the drawings.

1 *Marking a line at right angles to the edge of a piece of wood.*

2 *Marking the centre of a hole to be drilled in a piece of metal.*

3 *Marking a radius on the corner of a piece of acrylic.*

Check the facts

Measuring very accurately is sometimes required, especially when working with metal, where it may be necessary to measure to 0.01 mm. Two tools are used for this accurate measuring – **vernier callipers** and **micrometers**.

A **vernier calliper** has a fixed scale divided up into millimetres and a sliding scale which has a distance of 49 millimetres divided up into 50 divisions. Therefore, each division on the sliding scale is 0.01 mm smaller than a full millimetre. This allows measurements to 0.1mm to be taken. See diagram 1 below.

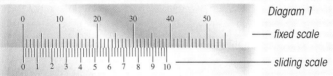

Diagram 1

— fixed scale

— sliding scale

To read the vernier, count the number of whole millimetres before the zero on the sliding scale. Then find the first line on the sliding scale which intersects with a line on the fixed scale. This will give the fraction. Add the two numbers to get the reading.

A **micrometer** has a revolving sleeve that turns on a screw thread with a pitch of 0.5 mm. One full turn will move the spindle a distance of 0.5 mm. The sleeve is divided into 50 divisions. Moving the sleeve 1 division will move the spindle $\frac{1}{50}$ of 0.5 mm = 0.01 mm. See diagram 2 below.

To read the micrometer, count the number of whole millimetres before the end of the revolving sleeve. Check for 0.5 mm divisions as well. Then add the number of divisions from the scale on the sleeve up to the datum line.

datum line

Diagram 2

— sleeve

Test yourself

Work out the vernier and micrometer calliper readings shown in the drawings.

1

2

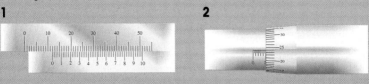

Cutting, shaping and joining materials

BBC GCSE Check and Test: Resistant Materials

Check the facts

Metal can be fabricated using components such as rivets and screwed fastenings.

Using rivets

There are two types of rivets. **Hammered rivets** are the traditional way of joining metal. To use a hammered rivet, a hole is drilled through the parts to be joined. The hole must be countersunk if a flat surface is needed. A rivet is put into the hole and hammered over. You need to be able to get to both sides of the product to use a hammered rivet, since the head must be supported whilst hammering.

Pop rivets are used where you can only get to one side of the component. A hole is drilled in both parts to be joined and the pop rivet is fitted into a special pair of pliers and put into the hole. Squeezing the pliers expands the end of the rivet and the pin snaps off.

Types of rivets

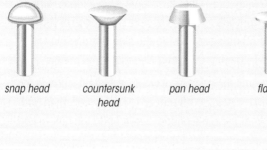

snap head   countersunk   pan head   flat head
head

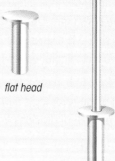

pop rivet

Test yourself

Name two products where rivets could be used to join parts together.

Metals

www.bbc.co.uk/revision

Check the facts

Metal can be fabricated using components screwed fastenings.

Screwed fastenings are machine screws, set screws, nuts and bolts, and self-tapping screws. They can be fitted into a plain hole and held in place with a nut, or fitted into a threaded hole. Self-tapping screws cut their own thread as they are screwed into the metal. They are normally used on thin sheet material.

Types of screwed fastenings

round
head

countersunk
head

pan
head

hexagon head
set screw

hexagon
head bolt

self tapping
screw

 Test yourself

Name suitable threaded fastenings for the following situations:

1 fixing the outside casing of a washing machine

2 fixing adjustable metal shelving together.

Metals

BBC GCSE Check and Test: Resistant Materials

Check the facts

Screw threads can be made on metal and some plastics.

A screw thread is made in a hole, using a tap that is held in a tap holder. The size of the hole drilled is smaller than the size of the screw thread, since you need to cut into the side of the hole.

A screw thread is made on a metal rod using a circular split die held in a die stock. The rod needs to be the same size as the size of the screw thread.

The drawings below show the process of screw threading and list the tapping sizes for common metric threads. Self-tapping screws cut their own thread and are usually only used on thin materials.

Taps and dies

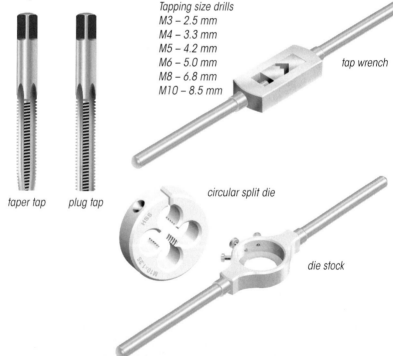

Tapping size drills
M3 – 2.5 mm
M4 – 3.3 mm
M5 – 4.2 mm
M6 – 5.0 mm
M8 – 6.8 mm
M10 – 8.5 mm

tap wrench

taper tap   plug tap

circular split die

die stock

Test yourself

1 State the drill size to be used for a hole to take an M5 thread.

2 Which tap should be used to finish a screw thread in a hole which does not go all the way through a piece of metal.

Metals

Check the facts

Metal can be joined by soldering or welding.

Soldering uses heat and an alloy of metal to make the joint. The solder forms an alloy with the metal being joined. A **flux** is used to keep the metal clean and prevent oxides from forming whilst the metal is heated.

Soft soldering is done using a solder made from lead and tin. Some modern solders are now lead free. The flux can be zinc chloride or rosin. The work is heated using a soldering iron. The most common form of soft soldering is the joining of electrical and electronic components, but lead, copper and brass can also be joined by soft soldering. The temperature required for soft soldering is about 340° C.

Hard soldering includes brazing and silver soldering. Hard soldering is done using a gas/air blow torch and requires a much higher temperature than soft soldering. Brazing is done using brazing spelter, which is an alloy of copper and zinc. Normally brazing is used to join mild steel and needs a temperature of about 880° C.

Silver soldering is usually used to join copper, brass and silver.
There are three grades of silver solder, details of these are shown in the chart below.

Copper	Silver	Copper	Zinc	Approx. melting point
Hard	80%	20%		780 – 825°C
Medium	75%	20%	5%	780 – 775°C
Easy	50%	30%	20%	690 – 740°C

Rules for a good soldered joint

• The surfaces of the metal must be clean. Remove oil and any oxide with emery cloth.

• The joint must fit closely together.

• The metal must be heated to the correct temperature.

Test yourself

Name a method of soldering suitable for the following situations and say why they are used:

1 joining wires in an electrical circuit

2 joining the parts of a shelf bracket made from mild steel.

Metals

BBC GCSE Check and Test: Resistant Materials

Check the facts

> Welding is used to join two or more pieces of the same sort of metal. Welding works by melting and fusing the two parts together.

A filler rod of the same metal is used to give a smooth joint or to strengthen the joint. Metal to be welded is heated by a gas flame or an electric current. Flux is usually needed to keep the metal clean and prevent oxides forming.

Oxy-acetylene

In oxy-acetylene or gas welding, oxygen and acetylene are mixed together in a blowpipe and used to heat the metal. The metal melts and fuses together. A filler rod is used to add extra metal if needed. Mild steel can be welded using this method. The temperature needed is about 1400° C.

Manual metal arc (MMA)

In this method, a filler rod, which is coated with a flux, is placed in a holder that is connected to a source of electric current. The work is connected to the same source. When the welding rod touches the work an electric current passes through the work piece and heats it sufficiently to melt the metal. The filler rod is used to provide additional metal.

Manual inert gas (MIG)

MIG welding is a similar process to MMA welding. The filler rod is in the form of a coil of wire, which is fed through the holder. A gas, usually argon for mild steel, is used to prevent the formation of oxides. This means that rods coated in flux are not needed. MMA and MIG welding are mainly used to weld mild steel, but other metals can be welded using these methods, if the correct filler rods and shielding gases are used.

Test yourself

Outline the process of gas welding using oxygen and acetylene.

Metals

Check the facts

Casting

Sand casting uses a pattern nromally made from wood. The pattern must be smooth and include the main details of the component. It must have tapered sides to allow it to be removed from the mould. The pattern is put in a moulding box or flask and fine sand is packed tightly around the mould. The sand is made to stick together using water or oil.

When the mould is finished, the pattern is removed and holes made to allow the molten metal to be poured in and the air to escape. When the metal has cooled, the casting is removed from the sand mould. Sand casting can be used for one-off jobs or for a small batch.

Die casting uses a metal mould which can include very fine detail. The mould is made in two parts to allow the casting to be removed. Die casting is used for mass production jobs.

Lost wax casting uses a wax pattern that can be carved into shape. It can include fine detail and because of this it is often used for jewellery. The wax pattern is covered with plaster and the wax is melted out. The metal is then poured in. When the metal has cooled, the plaster is broken away. Lost wax casting can only be used for a one-off job.

Test yourself

Describe the process of sand casting.

Metals

BBC GCSE Check and Test: Resistant Materials

Check the facts

A drilling machine can be used to make holes in wood, metal and plastics materials. The advantages of using the drilling machine are:

- holes will always be at right angles to the surface of the material
- more power is available than using a portable electric drill.

Types of drill bit and the materials which they are normally used on are shown in the drawings below.

twist drill – can be used on metal, plastics and wood

flat bit – used mainly on wood

saw tooth bit – used on wood, plastics and soft metals

Holding work

The work piece needs to be held firmly in place when drilling holes. Thin sheet metal and plastics material should be held in a **hand vice** or clamped to the worktable with a **clamp**. Thicker pieces of material should be held in a **machine vice**. The vice should be bolted or clamped to the worktable. Large pieces of material can be held by hand or clamped directly to the worktable. Put a scrap piece of wood underneath the work when drilling a hole all the way through a piece of material.

Safety when using the drilling machine

- A chuck guard must be fitted to the machine and used.
- Eye protection must be used.
- Protective clothing must be worn.
- Tie long hair back and secure loose clothing.
- The drill bit must be tightly held in the chuck.
- Ensure that the chuck key is removed before starting the machine.
- The work must be held firmly.
- Only the operator should start the machine.
- Other people should not come within one metre of the machine when it is being used.
- Remove waste materials with a rake or brush.

Test yourself

1 Name a drill bit suitable for drilling a 6 mm diameter hole in metal.

2 Name a drill bit suitable for drilling a 20 mm diameter hole in wood.

Check the facts

A metal turning lathe **can be used for a wide range of tasks. The lathe is the easiest way of making a hole in the end of a round bar.**

The work piece is held in a **chuck**. A **three jaw self-centering chuck** is used for round and hexagonal bars. A **four jaw independent chuck** is used for square bars, irregular shapes and round bars if the work has to be very accurate.

Drilling

A centre drill is used first since it will always find the exact centre of the work piece. Hold the centre drill in the tail stock chuck, move the tail stock up to the work and clamp it to the bed. Turn the hand wheel on the tail stock to drill the hole. Only drill as far as the slope of the end of the centre drill. Replace the centre drill with a standard twist drill to make the hole.

Safety when using the lathe

- A chuck guard must be fitted to the machine and used.
- Eye protection must be used.
- Protective clothing must be worn.
- Tie long hair back and secure loose clothing.
- The work must be held firmly.
- Ensure that the chuck key is removed before starting the machine.
- Only the operator should start the machine.
- Other people should not come within 1 metre of the machine when it is being used.
- Remove waste materials with a rake or brush.

Test yourself

Which component should be used to start the hole when drilling a hole in the end of a round bar?

Metals

BBC GCSE Check and Test: Resistant Materials

Check the facts

The metal turning lathe can be used to reduce the diameter of round bars. This is called parallel turning.

Hold the work in the chuck. If the part to be turned down is long, the outer end should be supported on the tail stock centre. A centre hole, made with a centre drill, should be made first. Reduce the diameter in small stages using the cross slide hand wheel to put on the cut. Check the diameter with outside calipers, vernier calipers or outside micrometer.

Parallel turning – reducing diameter of a piece of metal

direction of cutting tool

The metal turning lathe can be used to smooth the end of round bars or other components. This is called facing.

Hold the work in the chuck, as close in to the chuck as possible. Take cuts across the surface of the work. Use the apron hand wheel to put on the cut and the cross slide to remove the material.

Facing – smoothing the end of a piece of metal

direction of cutting tool

Test yourself

Sketch the processes of:
1 parallel turning
2 facing.

Metals

Check the facts

There are four heat treatment processes that you need to know about.

Annealing – softens the metal by heating and allowing to cool slowly. All metals can be annealed. For copper and brass, the metal should be heated to a dull red heat of about 700° C. Normalising is similar to annealing and is applied to low carbon steel. The metal is allowed to cool in air.

Hardening – the process of changing the state of medium and high carbon steel. The metal is heated to bright red, about 750° C, and cooled quickly in water. The steel becomes hard and brittle.

Tempering – the process of taking away some of the brittleness. The metal is heated until the tempering colours appear and then cooled quickly in water. The steel becomes tough as well as hard. Hardening and tempering can only be done on medium and high carbon steel.

Tempering colours	Temperature
Dark blue	300° C
Dark purple	280° C
Purple	260° C
Brown	240° C
Dark straw	220° C
Light straw	300° C

Case hardening – the process of creating a hard skin on mild steel. The metal is heated to bright red, about 880° C, and dipped into a carbon rich substance. It is then heated and cooled in water. The process can be repeated several times to increase the thickness of the skin. This process can only be done on low carbon steels.

Test yourself

1 List the metals that can be hardened and tempered.

2 Give examples of products that would need to be hardened and tempered.

Metals

BBC GCSE Check and Test: Resistant Materials

Check the facts

When designing and making, you can save time and effort if you make use of standard sizes of metal and standard components.

Metals come in a range of standard sizes of bars and sheets. Unless a special size is needed, always try to make use of these standard sizes. Use a catalogue to check the standard sizes that are available.

When choosing materials you need to:

- Match the materials available to the desired shape or form needed. For example, buy an angle section of metal rather than bending a piece of sheet metal or machining from a solid square bar.

- Match the materials available to the manufacturing processes available. Aluminium can be welded using a MIG welder. If you do not have these skills, or the equipment is not available, it is not sensible to specify the process.

- Ensure minimum waste. When ordering materials or when marking out and cutting, plan in advance. Try to ensure that left-over pieces, after marking out lengths, can be used for another component.

Standard components, such as threaded fastenings, also come in standard sizes of diameter and length. Always try to make use of these. Again, you can use a catalogue to check standard sizes when planning.

Test yourself

The drawing shows a simple book rack made from mild steel, which is then painted. Work out how to cut the various pieces from standard 3 metre lengths of bar.

All parts made from 8 mm diameter mild steel. All dimensions in millimetres.

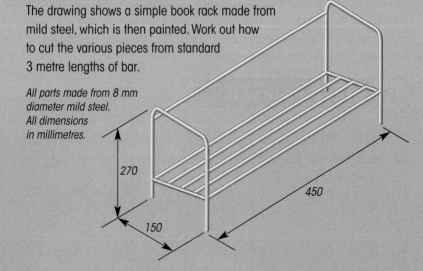

270

450

150

Check the facts

There are three main types of construction using wood. These are:

- **Flat frame construction**, which might be used to make a box to be covered with thin sheet material.

- **Three-dimensional frame construction**, such as a small table or frame of a stool or cupboard.

- **Carcase or box construction**, which might be used to make a box or cupboard.

The way in which these types of construction are made, and the materials and joints that are used, will differ depending on the job. Sometimes different methods of construction will be used on the same job.

Topic 58 shows the joints that can be used for the different methods of construction.

Test yourself

This drawing shows two different wood-based products.

Name the types of construction used on the products.

Small cupboard with 3D frame base

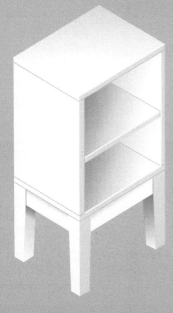

Cupboard with carcase body, plinth and framed door

Wood and wood-based materials

BBC GCSE Check and Test: Resistant Materials

Wood and wood-based materials

Check the facts

Wood can be fabricated using components such as nails, screws and knock down fittings.

Using nails and pins

Nails are generally used where appearance is not important, or where a quick job is needed. **Panel pins** and **veneer pins** are used to fix backs onto cupboards and bottoms onto boxes. Veneer pins are finer than panel pins. Nails and pins are usually made of mild steel, but brass and copper nails and pins are available for special work.

Types of nails

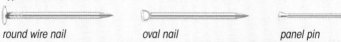

round wire nail   oval nail   panel pin

Wood screws

Wood screws are used to give a strong joint, to fix things that may need to be taken apart, or to fix metal components to wood. Wood screws can be made of mild steel or brass.

Types of screws

round head wood screw   countersunk head wood screw

Knock down fittings

Knock down fittings (KD fittings) are made of metal or plastic and are designed to enable products made of wood to be taken apart easily.

A stronger joint that can be separated by undoing the machine screw.

Examples of knock down fittings

Knock down fitting fixed with wood screws to two adjacent panels.

Test yourself

Name a fabrication method suitable for the following situations:

1 construction of a flat pack bookcase

2 fixing wheels to a wooden toy

3 fixing the back to a bedside cupboard.

www.bbc.co.uk/revision

Check the facts

Wood can be joined by cutting joints or by using other components.

Flat-frame joints

Corner halving joint

Cross halving joint

Dowel joint

Three-dimensional frame joints

Bridle joint

Mortice and tenon joint

Haunch mortice and tenon joint

Carcase or box joints

Lap joint

Through dovetail joint

Stopped housing joint

Test yourself

Name a type of joint suitable for the following processes:

1 fitting shelves into a bookcase

2 joining the legs to the frame of a stool

3 making a frame for a display board.

Check the facts

Some types of solid timber can be bent into shapes by **steam bending**. The timber is put into a container and steam is passed through it, which softens the timber so that it can be bent into shape. The best timber for steam bending is ash. Little use is made of steam bending today.

For more complex shapes, **laminating** is used. This is easier to do than steam bending and can be done using many different types of timber. A mould is first made to give the required shape. This is normally made in two parts – male and female. The wood is cut into thin strips, normally about 1.5 mm thick, but this depends on the sharpnesss of the curve. Glue is applied and the strips put into the mould and held by clamps until the glue dries.

Thin plywood can be used for laminating, rather than cutting thin strips of solid timber. A vacuum bag press can be used instead of one half of a mould. Air pressure is used to apply pressure until the glue dries. Laminating cannot normally be used to make three-dimensional bends.

Test yourself

The drawing shows two different wood-based products. Give reasons why one would not be suitable for laminating.

Wooden bowl *Upright chair*

Check the facts

- When designing and making, you can save time and effort if you make use of standard sizes of wood and wood-based products.

- Wood comes in a range of standard sizes for square and rectangular softwood sections and some hardwood sections. Unless a special size is needed, always try to make use of these standard sizes.

- Lengths can vary but usually four metres is a standard length for softwood timber.

- Sheet materials, such as plywood and MDF, come in standard thicknesses and sheet sizes.

It is fairly easy to cut wood to size and to plane it smooth using woodworking machines. However, this can create a lot of waste material. Therefore, use standard sizes where possible. When marking out, it may be necessary to avoid knots and splits which may spoil the finished product.

Test yourself

This drawing shows a table made of softwood. The top is cut from birch plywood and an edging strip applied. The top is not shown in the drawing. Use the information from topic 40 to work out the best way to mark out the lengths of wood needed if the wood is in two-metre lengths.

Table frame
Rails from 70 x 20 finished size
Legs from 45 x 45 finished size
All dimensions in millimetres

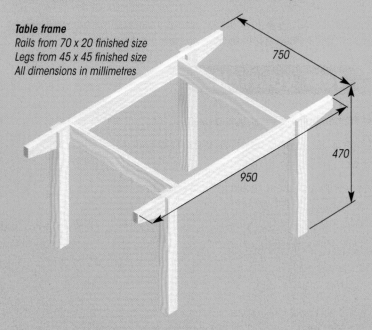

750

470

950

Wood and wood-based materials

BBC GCSE Check and Test: Resistant Materials

Wood and wood-based materials

Check the facts

There is a wide variety of hinges and other metal fittings for use on wood.

The drawings below show a range of hinges and other components used with wood and common applications.

Butt hinge – used for general purpose work.

Piano hinge – used where support is needed along the whole length of the moving section. Available in lengths up to 2 metres long.

Back flap hinge – used for narrow pieces of wood or where more support is needed, e.g. folding tables.

Surface fitting lock – a lock that is screwed to the inside surface of a door. Easy to fit but not very neat.

Cut cupboard lock – a recess is needed to take the lock. Gives a neater appearance.

Box lock with catch plate – special lock for boxes with hinged lids.

Test yourself

Name the components that could be used in the following products:

1 a hinge for an opening bookcase that can be folded shut when not required

2 a lock for the cupboard shown in topic 56.

www.bbc.co.uk/revision

Check the facts

Plastics materials can be shaped by wasting techniques. For most plastics, metalworking tools are used, although a coping saw can cut curves in acrylic and other plastics provided that the material is not too thin.

Drilling acrylic

- Clamp the work firmly to the drilling machine table.
- Put scrap wood under the work piece to support it.
- Use the correct drilling speed.
- Using drill bits with a special point angle gives the best results.

Finishing acrylic

- Use a smooth file to draw file the edges to remove scratches.
- Use silicon carbide (wet and dry) abrasive paper after draw filing.
- Polish with metal polish or on the buffing machine.

Test yourself

This drawing shows a simple pendant made from layers of acrylic glued together.

1 How would the shape be cut?

2 How would the surfaces be smoothed?

3 How should the hole be made?

Plastics and composite materials

BBC GCSE Check and Test: Resistant Materials

Plastics and composite materials

Check the facts

> The main ways of fabricating plastics are by using adhesives and threaded fastenings.
> Rivets can be used but only if great care is taken.

Adhesives

Tensol No. 12 is the most common adhesive for acrylics. It works by dissolving the two surfaces and fusing them together. Joints must fit closely together and be held together until the adhesive hardens.

Liquid polystyrene cement

This is a thin liquid that will also dissolve the joining surfaces. It is mainly used on polystyrene but can also be used on acrylic. Again, joints must fit closely together and be held together until the adhesive hardens.

Screwed fastenings

Screw threads can be cut in acrylic using standard taps. Clearance holes can be drilled and the work joined with machine screws and nuts.

Rivets

Hammered rivets can be used to joint acrylic. For best results, use rivets made of aluminium and make sure that the holes are not too close to the edge of the material.

Test yourself

These drawings show two ways of joining acrylic using an adhesive.

Which joint would be the strongest? Explain your answer.

Butt joint

Lap joint

www.bbc.co.uk/revision

Check the facts

Deforming of plastics can be done by line bending, press forming and vacuum forming.

Line bending

The work is heated on a strip heater or a line-bending machine. A strip heater uses an infra-red heating element to heat the plastic. A line-bending machine uses a length of resistance wire to do the heating. Normally, acrylic and polystyrene are bent in this way. The work is heated until soft and bent to the required angle.

Press forming

A mould is made in two halves – male and female. Allowance must be made for the thickness of the material and for deforming of the waste material. The plastic is heated in an oven and placed in the mould. Pressure is then applied to force the plastic into shape.

Vacuum forming

A mould is made, usually in wood, which must be smooth and have tapering sides to allow the formed plastic to be removed. The mould is placed in the vacuum forming machine and the plastic sheet clamped in a frame. Heat is applied. When the material is soft, in a plastic state, a vacuum is created under the sheet. Air pressure pushes the plastic sheet over the mould.

Test yourself

The drawing shows two products that could be made in a school or college workshop.

Name the processes that could be used to shape these products.

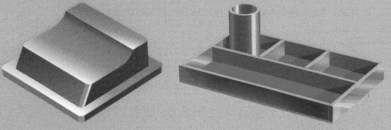

Box for electronic circuit   *Simple desk tidy*

Plastics and composite materials

Check the facts

Polyester resin can be used in conjunction with glass fibre or carbon fibre to produce strong shapes in two or three dimensions. If combined with glass fibre, the technique is known as glass reinforced plastic (GRP).

Making a product using GRP

- A mould is made of the shape required. This can be made from wood or from GRP. The mould must be made very smooth, since bumps and scratches will come out on the moulding.

- Polish the mould surface and apply a release agent.

- Mix gel coat resin with a colour pigment, add catalyst and brush onto the mould. Allow to harden. Filler powder may be added to the resin, if required, in place of colour pigment.

- Line the mould with glass fibre mat, add catalyst to lay-up resin and stipple into the mat. Allow to harden. Repeat as required.

- When resin has hardened, remove from the mould and trim up.

Test yourself

Research the safety measures needed when working with GRP.

Check the facts

> Plastics materials can be formed into complex shapes by injection moulding. The process is used extensively in industry.

- A mould is made in metal, usually in two halves with locating pegs to make sure that it is assembled the right way round. For round components, the mould is split along the centre line of the component. A hole is made to allow plastic to be forced into the mould.

- The mould is placed in the injection moulding machine. Plastic granules are heated in the machine until they fuse together in a paste-like consistency.

- A nozzle is moved up to the entry hole of the mould and the plastic forced into the machine under high pressure.

- When the plastic is cooled, the moulding is removed.

Common injection moulded products

Toys, especially construction kits, such as model aircraft kits, handles of tools, small gears, keys of computer keyboards, casings for electrical and electronic equipment.

Test yourself

The drawing shows a simple pulley wheel that could be made by injection moulding. Sketch one half of the mould to show the space into which the plastic would be forced.

Plastics and composite materials

Check the facts

Products made of plastics materials that are in the form of long strips, but which have complex shapes, can be formed into complex shapes by extrusion.

The process of extrusion is used extensively in industry. Examples of extruded products include curtain rails and the frames for replacement windows. Plastic can also be extruded onto other materials such as metal wire.

- A die is made in metal. The die has a shaped hole in it that is the shape of the finished product.

- The die is placed in the machine. Plastic granules are heated in the machine until they fuse together in a paste-like consistency.

- The softened plastic is forced through the hole in the die. It will take on the form of the hole and retain it while it cools.

Test yourself

Name three products that could be made by extrusion.

www.bbc.co.uk/revision

Check the facts

When designing and making, you can save time and effort if you make use of standard sizes of plastics and standard components.

Acrylic is available in a range of standard sizes of rods, tubes, sheets and colours. Unless a special size is needed, always try to make use of these standard sizes.

Polystyrene is available mainly in sheets for vacuum forming. If designing something to be made by vacuum forming you need to make sure that there is room in the machine for the mould and to form the material.

Polystyrene and PVC are also available in extruded forms as tube and angle sections. Nylon and other engineering plastics are available in round and square rods, and in tube form.

When choosing materials, remember the following:

- Use the standard sizes of materials. Solid shapes may be machined to size on a lathe or milling machine.
- If colours are important, check that the required colours are available.

Test yourself

The drawing shows a simple box made from a plastics material glued together. Work out the best way of cutting the parts from a sheet of acrylic that is 400 mm square and 5 mm thick.

When the lid is fitted on to the base, the box forms a cube. Each side is 150 mm square. The box is made as a cube and the lid is cut off when the glue has set.

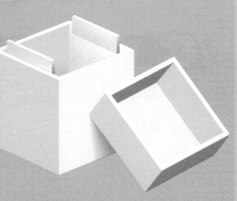

Plastics and composite materials

BBC GCSE Check and Test: Resistant Materials

Check the facts

Modern materials are defined as those that have been developed in the last 25 years or so. The term **smart materials** is sometimes used to describe some of these materials where their physical properties can vary when an external force, such as an electric current or a magnetic force, acts as an input.

Types of smart materials

Shape memory alloys, for example, Nitinol is an alloy of nickel and titanium. When heated by an electric current, the metal contracts and when the current is removed, the metal returns to its original length. A thin wire of about 2 mm diameter can exert a force of 10 Newtons when contracting by 5% of its original length.

Piezo-electric ceramics expand and contract when a voltage is applied. They have possible applications in loud speakers.

Optical fibres have a traditional use as a lighting effect. Now frequently used in telecommunications and computer technology for the transmission of data.

Photochromic glass is a type of glass which contains silver-halide. When exposed to ultra-violet light the glass changes colour and blocks out ultra-violet light. Used in sunglasses and welding goggles.

Test yourself

Suggest an application of smart memory alloy to a Design and Technology product.

Check the facts

> The majority of plastics materials have been developed over the last 40 years. However, some plastics have only recently come into existence.

Types of modern plastics materials

Low temperature setting plastic, for example, Polymorph. This material can be shaped when heated to about 70° C.

Closed cell sheet material, for example, Plastazote. A sheet material with a cell-like structure similar to the foam used in upholstery. It may be shaped by heating to about 70° C and formed into 3D shapes.

Reinforcement of plastics

Many plastics materials are brittle. Polyester resin is one of these. It can be reinforced by the use of glass fibre or carbon fibre, both of which are available in the form of loosely woven mats or as mats of short chopped strands.

Kevlar is a composite material based on carbon fibre.

Uses for modern plastics

Polymorph – prototype models, especially for things like tool handles, when it can be moulded by hand without the risk of burning.

Plastazote – forming 3D shapes such as masks and as the basis for clothing.

Glass reinforced plastics – boat building, panels for motor vehicles, storage tanks for liquids.

Carbon reinforced plastics – fishing rods, uses in the aerospace industries, sports equipment.

Test yourself

Suggest an application of Polymorph to a Design and Technology product.

New materials

BBC GCSE Check and Test: Resistant Materials

Check the facts

When used in a product, a system is a set of components arranged to carry out a particular function.

Systems can consist of mechanical, electrical, electronic, pneumatic or hydraulic components. Some systems will combine components from more than one of these groups.

Systems consist of separate sections – **input**, **process** and **output**. Many systems also involve the use of **feedback**.

The **input** is what goes into the system. In a music centre, the input comes from a record or CD player, a radio tuner and a tape player. The **process** part of a music centre is the amplifier. The **output** is the speakers connected to the amplifier. **Feedback** is used to set the volume. If the music is too loud, the user will reduce the volume. If the radio tuner is not set to the required station, the user will adjust it.

In some systems, the action of one part of one system will cause another system to function – a special form of feedback.

Test yourself

The drawing shows a simple toy that includes two different systems which are connected to each other.

1 Name the two types of system.

2 Name the two components that form the connecting element of the system.

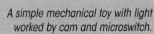

A simple mechanical toy with light worked by cam and microswitch.

Systems and control

Check the facts

It is possible to analyse a system to identify the inputs, processes and outputs and where feedback occurs.

Analysis of a mechanical system

You need to look at the system to identify the input, process and output. In the system shown in topic 71, the operating handle is the input, the cam is the process and the moving figure is the output. There is no feedback involved in operating the system, but when it is put together and operated for the first time, feedback would be obtained by seeing how far the figures moved, and if the cam hit the sides of the supporting frame.

A mechanical system can also be used to change the direction of the movement for the output and change the amount of force for the output.

If the output speed is **increased** compared with the input speed, then the output force is reduced when compared with the input force.

If the output speed is **decreased** compared with the input speed, then the output force is increased when compared with the input force.

You cannot have a fast speed and a high output force together.

Test yourself

Work out the inputs, processes and outputs shown in the systems illustrated below.

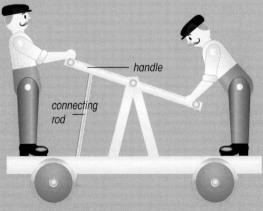

handle

connecting rod

The two figures move up and down as the cam moves the connecting rod.

Systems and control

- To design your own system, firstly decide what is the output required. This will probably be some sort of motion – linear, rotary, reciprocating or oscillating (see topic 74). You also need to decide on the force required for the output.
- Then decide what the input motion will be – again, one of the four types of motion given.
- You can now make a decision about the process part of the system. This could involve the use of levers, cams, cranks, pulleys or gears (see topics 77–79). The direction of the movement may also have to be changed.

Other design decisions

- How can moving parts be supported – what sort of bearings will be needed?
- Will the systems be hand powered or powered by a small motor?
- How can friction be overcome?
- What is the degree of accuracy required?

Once these decisions have been made, you can design it on paper and model it before making it in suitable materials.

Test yourself

The drawing below shows part of an automaton or mechanical toy.

Decide what mechanical systems should be used to give the required movements.

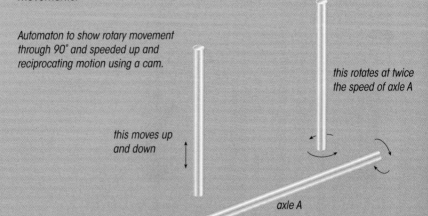

Automaton to show rotary movement through 90° and speeded up and reciprocating motion using a cam.

this rotates at twice the speed of axle A

this moves up and down

axle A

Check the facts

Types of motion

There are four types of motion that can be used in mechanical systems:

Rotary motion – turning round in a circle, e.g. a wheel turning.

Linear motion – moving in a straight line, e.g. on a paper trimmer.

Reciprocating motion – moving backwards and forwards in a straight line, e.g. cutting with a saw.

Oscillating motion – swinging from side to side, e.g. a pendulum in a clock.

Changing the direction of motion

These types of motion can be changed into another type by the use of mechanisms. The chart below gives a summary of these methods of changing motion.

Type of change	Mechanism to use
Linear to rotary and rotary to linear	Wheel and axle, rack and pinion, rope and pulley, screw thread
Rotary to reciprocating	Crank, link and slider, cam and follower
Reciprocating to rotary	Crank, link and slider
Rotary to oscillating	Crank, link and slider, cam and follower, peg and slot
Oscillating to rotary	Crank, link and slider, peg and slot
Reciprocating to oscillating	Rack and pinion, crank, link and slider
Oscillating to reciprocating	Crank, link and slider, cam and follower

Test yourself

Name the mechanisms that could be used in the following situations:

1 The mechanism to move a CD drive in and out on a computer.

2 The mechanism that moves the seat of a swivel chair up and down when the seat is turned round.

3 The mechanism that moves an electric fan from side to side.

BBC GCSE Check and Test: Resistant Materials

Systems and control

Check the facts

The direction of movement and the amount of speed and force transmitted can be altered. Note that the force and speed cannot both be increased. You can have high speeds and low force, or low speeds and high force.

The chart below gives a summary of the methods of changing direction, speed and force.

Type of change	Mechanism to use
From clockwise to anti-clockwise	Equal number of gears, pulley and crossed belt
From left to right	One lever or linked levers
From vertical to horizontal	One lever or linked levers
Change axis of rotation	Pulley and crossed belt, bevel gears, worm and worm wheel
To increase output force and decrease speed	Straight line movement – use one lever or linked levers. Rotary movement – use belt and pulley, gears, bevel gears, chain and sprocket, worm and worm wheel. In all cases the **driver** component must be **smaller** than the **driven** component.
To decrease output force and increase speed	Straight line movement – use one lever or linked levers. Rotary movement – use belt and pulley, gears, bevel gears, chain and sprocket. In all cases the **driver** component must be **larger** than the **driven** component.

Test yourself

Name the mechanisms that could be used in the following situations:

1 To change the direction of rotary movement from clockwise to anti-clockwise.

2 To change the axis of rotation when a slow speed is needed.

3 To give a fast speed and low force between two axles 600 mm apart.

Check the facts

> A lever is a rigid piece of material that turns about a fixed point. The fixed point is called the fulcrum.

An input force (the **effort**) applied to one end of a lever will be transmitted to the other end of the lever to move the output force (the **load**). If the input and output forces of a lever are the same the lever should not move.

Levers can change:

- where you apply a force
- how much force is needed
- the direction of movement
- the amount of movement.

The fulcrum of a lever does not have to be in the middle. If the fulcrum is nearer to the load, then a large load can be moved with a small effort. The distance travelled by the effort is greater than the distance travelled by the load.

If the fulcrum is nearer to the effort, then a small load will need a larger effort to move it. The distance travelled by the effort is smaller than the distance travelled by the load.

Test yourself

Drawings of lever systems used in resistant materials products are shown below.

1 Identify the types of lever system used in each diagram.

2 Show the load and effort on each lever.

Check the facts

- Levers are used to transmit a force from one place to another.

- A set of levers is called a linkage.

- Linkages can be used in a number of different products, such as adjustable lamps, mechanical toys, vehicle jacks and other products with moving parts.

Design decisions about levers

- How much force has to be transmitted – what is the amount of load and effort?

- What is the direction of the output force compared to the input force?

- Which class of lever will be used? What are the relative positions of load, fulcrum and effort?

- What material will the lever be made from? Is the material sufficiently rigid and strong?

- How will the fulcrum be made and supported?

- How will the effort be applied? By hand or by mechanical means?

Test yourself

The drawings below show two design situations where lever systems could be used to provide the desired movement. Draw a possible solution to each situation.

View from back

1 Design a lever system to move the ears when the lever at the bottom is pulled down.

2 Design a lever system to make the legs of the tortoise move in **opposite** directions when the tail is moved in and out.

Systems and control

www.bbc.co.uk/revision

Check the facts

- A **pulley wheel** is a wheel with a groove round the outside to take a driving belt.

- Pulleys are used to transmit rotary movement from one place to another.

- The axles for pulleys can be parallel or at an angle.

- Pulleys can transmit motion over a considerable distance by using only two pulleys.

- An **open driving belt** will cause two pulleys to turn in the same direction.

- A **crossed driving belt** will cause two pulleys to turn in opposite directions.

- A driving belt turned through an angle can be used when the axles are not parallel.

- Traditional driving belts can slip. Modern toothed pulley wheels and belts will not slip, but the belts cannot be crossed or angled.

Design decisions about pulleys

- How much power has to be transmitted?

- How will the axles be supported? What will the bearings be made from?

- How will the power be applied? By hand or by mechanical means?

- What material will be used for the driving belt?

- Will bought-in components be used or will the pulleys be made?

Test yourself

The drawings below show two design situations where pulley systems could be used to provide the desired movement. Draw a possible solution to each situation.

— motor

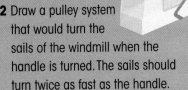

1 Draw a pulley system that would allow the motor to turn the vertical rod. The rod should turn three times slower than the motor.

2 Draw a pulley system that would turn the sails of the windmill when the handle is turned. The sails should turn twice as fast as the handle.

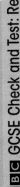

Systems and control

BBC GCSE Check and Test: Resistant Materials

Check the facts

- A gear wheel is a wheel with teeth round the outside that lock into the teeth on an adjacent gear.

- The teeth are often called cogs.

- Types of gears include:
  spur gears – axles must be parallel
  bevel gears – axles can be at an angle to each other
  worm and worm wheel – axles must be at 90° to each other
  rack and pinion – a rack is a gear in a straight line.

- Gears are used to transmit rotary movement from one place to another.

- Gears are used to transmit motion over short distances.

- Two gears working together will turn in the same direction.

- If three gears are working together the ones on the ends will turn in the same direction.

- Gears will not slip.

Design decisions about gears

- How much power has to be transmitted?

- How will the axles be supported? What will the bearings be made from?

- How will the power be applied? By hand or by mechanical means?

Test yourself

The drawings below show two design situations where gear systems could be used to provide the desired movement. Draw a possible solution to each situation.

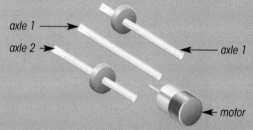

axle 1

axle 2

axle 1

motor

1 Show how spur gears could be used to connect the motor to the axles. Axle 1 should go four times slower than the motor. Axle 2 should go twice as fast as axle 1. Axle 3 should go three times slower than axle 1.

2 Which type of gear could be used to connect two axles at 90° to each other? One must turn at half the speed of the other.

Systems and control

Check the facts

When using tools and machines, look at the machine and check that it is working correctly, then make use of this feedback. When using jigs and templates, make sure that they are free of waste so that components can be fitted accurately into place.

Types of feedback indicators

Temperature gauges – usually digital
Light emitting diodes – different colours, steady and flashing
Visual display units – when using CNC machines, the monitor will show, through the software, if something is not correct.

Feed handles on machines, such as metal turning lathes and milling machines, are usually fitted with graduations that show the amount of movement made when the handle is turned.

Depth stops on drilling machines allow holes which do not go all the way through a piece of material to be made to a set depth.

Feedback indications from hand and machine tools

Feedback indication from hand and machine tools	Cause	Solution/action
Excessive noise	Cutting too quickly – by hand or machine. Work piece vibrating.	Slow down rate of cutting. Hold work in vice or clamp, or cut closer to point of support.
'Wrong' sort of noise from tools	Tools are blunt. Incorrect cutting speed.	Sharpen tools. Cut at correct speed.
Temperature (metals) Change in surface colour. Surface temperature increases.	Blunt cutting tools Speed too fast. Feed rate too quick.	Sharpen tools Cut at correct speed Feed tool at correct rate.
Temperature (plastics) Smoke or cracking of surface	Temperature of equipment too high. Material left in/on for too long.	Reduce temperature. Reduce time exposed to heat.

Test yourself

1 List three feedback indicators on equipment in the workshops at your school or college.

2 In what way does the operator have to respond?

Check the facts

- A drill bit should turn at the correct speed for the material and the size of the bit.

- As a general rule, the speed should reduce as the size of bit increases.

- Softer materials are drilled at higher speeds than harder materials.

- The rate at which the drill bit is fed into the work to make the hole should reduce as the size of drill bit increases.

- A drill bit needs to be kept sharp in order to do its job correctly.

- If a hole does not go all the way through a piece of material, the depth stop on the machine can be used to assist in drilling the hole to the correct depth.

Feedback signs to look for when drilling

Feedback signs	Cause	Remedy
Excessive heat when drilling any material, or even smoke when drilling wood	Speed too fast, feed rate too quick, blunt drill bit	Reduce speed, reduce feed, sharpen drill bit
Excessive noise, especially when drilling metals or plastics	Speed too fast, feed rate too quick, blunt drill bit	Reduce speed, reduce feed, sharpen drill bit
Difficulty in feeding the drill bit into the work	Blunt drill bit	Sharpen drill bit

Test yourself

The chart below shows some situations where holes are to be made in different materials. Decide on the drill speed (high, medium or low) for each situation.

Material	Size of hole	Speed
Mild steel	12 mm diameter	
Oak	25 mm diameter	
Acrylic	4 mm diameter	

Check the facts

When using a vacuum-forming machine:

- the mould has to be smooth
- the sides of the mould must slope inwards from bottom to top
- there should not be 'cut-ins' or reverse slopes on the mould
- the plastic must be formed at the correct temperature.

Feedback signs to look for when using a vacuum-forming machine

Feedback signs	Cause	Remedy
Smell of burning, fumes, smoke	Plastic is too hot	Reduce temperature or time exposed to heat
Plastic does not form over mould	Material too cool, poor seal or leaks of air	Heat the material for longer, check seals
Plastic does not release from mould	No taper, or undercut on mould, plastic too cool	Modify mould, remove mould earlier

Test yourself

List two actions to be taken if plastic does not form correctly in a vacuum-forming machine.

Systems and control

BBC GCSE Check and Test: Resistant Materials

Systems and control

Check the facts

Systems planning can be used especially when making a small batch of the product, or when making several parts that are the same.

You need to consider the following points about systems thinking when designing products:

- Where must parts be accurate and fit together?
- What are the tolerances? (How much smaller or bigger can the parts be and still be usable?)
- When do I need to make checks?
- How can the parts be checked?
- What equipment and/or systems can be used to assist in checking?

You need to include this sort of planning information in your design folder.

Test yourself

The drawing on the right shows a simple rack for CDs that is made from wood. Ten are to be made. The table below shows some of the checks that would have to be made when making and some of the production aids.

1 Decide if the degree of accuracy for these is high, medium or low.

2 When must the checks be made?

The first is done for you.

Production process	Type of check	When check is needed	Accuracy
Shaping ends – mark out using template.	Check finished shape with template – by eye.	1 – after cutting 2 –	Medium
Cutting base and back to length – use sawing jig.	Check length with gauge. Check jig is free of sawdust and saw guide is not worn.		
Cutting mortises for joint on mortising machine.	Check correct size of mortise chisel. Check correct position of mortise on wood.		

Check the facts

Ten of the components shown in the drawing below are needed. Jigs are used to ensure they are all the same size. The material is already the correct length and width.

A simple component – flat acrylic with four holes.

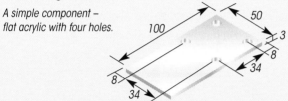

Two jigs are required to ensure that the strips are cut and finished to the correct length. A template will be required to ensure that the length is correct. Another jig will be needed to ensure that the holes are in the correct positions.

The chart shows the checks and when they will be made.

Check required	Tolerance	When checked	How checked
Finished length of part	Within 1.0 mm of required length	After cutting	Length template
Distance of holes from side and end	Within 0.5 mm of required distance	After drilling	With check gauge
Distance between holes – both directions	Within 0.5 mm of required distance	After drilling	With check gauge

The drawings below show an example of a template that could be made for checking the length of a component and a check gauge for checking the distance of the holes from the edges.

Gauge for checking length

Gauge for checking position of holes

Test yourself

Which feedback indicators could you use when making this component?

Systems and control

BBC GCSE Check and Test: Resistant Materials

Systems and control

Check the facts

> **A jig is defined as a device that assists in the making of a component, usually where a number are required which have to be identical.**

Jigs, formers, templates, patterns and moulds are all used to achieve identical parts. When designing a jig, you need to consider the following points:

- How the piece of material will be located, so that all pieces fit into the jig in the same way and in the same position.

- How the material will be held in the jig whilst the process is carried out.

- The disposal of waste, and making sure that waste does not affect the operation of the jig.

- How to ensure that parts of the jig do not wear away by the action of cutting tools, so that the jig becomes inaccurate.

- The degree of accuracy required.

If a jig is required for your course work, include the design and making of it in your design folder.

Test yourself

Look at the drawing of the component in topic 84.

1 How could you make sure that the material always fits into the right place in the jig?

2 How could you ensure that waste material can easily be removed from the jig?

Check the facts

Product design analysis involves a detailed examination of the following aspects of a product:

- The function and purpose of the product
- What the different parts of the product are and how they work together
- How the product actually works and any scientific principles involved
- The materials that are used to make the product
- The processes used to make the product
- The intended market for the product
- How well the product does its job when compared with other similar products.

Some of these aspects apply when looking at existing products before designing your own. In the GCSE, product design analysis is usually tested by looking at photographs or drawings of existing products and written information about them.

How to be successful at product design analysis

- Make sure that you understand what the product actually does and how it works.
- Learn carefully how products are made in industry – especially what sort of materials are usually used and how they are cut, shaped, formed, joined and finished. Apply this knowledge to the product you are asked to analyse.
- Think carefully about possible markets for different products. Who would buy the product? Why would they buy it? Where would it be used? Who would use the product?

Test yourself

The drawing on the right shows a two-hole paper punch.

1 Name the materials used for the base, the handle and the collecting tray.

2 Name the manufacturing processes that could be used to make these components.

Check the facts

There are two aspects to quality in Design and Technology:

- **quality of the design itself** – how well the product meets the needs of the user
- **quality of the manufacture** – how well the product has been made.

These two aspects of quality can be independent of each other. A product can be designed well but poorly made. A well-made product may be of a poor design which does not meet the needs of the user.

Example

A storage unit for books may be designed well but could be poorly made with rough edges, inaccurate cutting and poorly made joints. Alternatively, it could be well made but the shelves may be too thin to take the weight of the books, and they might be badly spaced so that books of different sizes do not fit into the spaces.

To ensure good quality in a product, the designer should ensure that:

- it meets the needs of the user
- appropriate materials are used
- where necessary, the product are capable of being maintained in good condition
- making is planned carefully to ensure that checks for quality are made at the appropriate time
- making is done carefully and accurately
- the use and disposal of the product after use have been considered.

Test yourself

The drawing on the right shows an electric fan.

1 State why you think the materials used for the main parts are appropriate.

2 Name two quality checks that could be made during making.

Products and quality

www.bbc.co.uk/revision

Check the facts

A quality product will meet fully the needs of the user. In order to ensure quality in meeting needs, find out exactly what the user requires. This can be done in a number of ways:

- talking to the user

- thinking carefully about what the user needs

- observing the user

- asking questions

- looking in books and magazines that illustrate the lifestyle of the user.

Not all of these points will be suitable for every situation. It may be difficult to talk to young children about what their needs are for different sorts of toys, but a designer could look at them at play and see what sort of toys they like to play with. A designer could, however, talk to parents or other adult helpers about what might be suitable.

Having identified exactly what the needs of the user are, they should be accurately recorded. When developing possible ideas, the designer should constantly refer back to the needs to ensure a quality product.

Test yourself

An airport departure lounge needs seats for the passengers.

1 List as many of the people who will use the seats as possible. Remember that someone has to buy them and keep them clean.

2 List the needs of the users of the seats.

Products and quality

BBC GCSE Check and Test: Resistant Materials

Check the facts

A quality product will use materials and components appropriately. In order to ensure quality in the use of materials and components, a designer needs to do the following things:

- make a list of the properties and qualities that the product requires the materials to possess

- collect information about materials and components that may have these properties, and samples that could be examined and tested

- carry out research into the properties and do tests on samples to see how closely they meet the requirements

- consider cost, working properties, maintenance and availability as part of the research and, where appropriate, what the user thinks

- make a decision based on all the relevant factors of the best materials and components for the purpose.

Test yourself

A child's pull-along toy on wheels could be made from:

- injection moulded polystyrene
- hardwood timber such as beech
- softwood timber such as pine.

List four aspects of these materials that should be considered when making a decision about which would be best to use from a quality point of view.

Check the facts

A quality product will be made using the most appropriate manufacturing processes and checks will be planned to ensure that manufacturing is of the best possible quality.

In order to ensure quality in manufacturing, a designer needs to do the following things:

- research the most effective ways of working the materials which will be used

- check to ensure that those involved in the making have the necessary equipment and skills to do the manufacturing to the agreed level of quality

- ensure that those involved in the making are aware of the degree of quality required for the product

- devise and use checks on quality at regular intervals or at critical points in the making processes

- ensure that bought-in components are made to the required quality level and are checked

- ensure that the cost of the final product is sufficient to meet the quality standards of making which are proposed

- make a decision based on all the relevant factors of the best methods to be used.

Test yourself

A child's pull-along toy on wheels could be made from:

- injection moulding polystyrene
- cutting and shaping hardwood timber mainly by hand methods
- cutting and shaping softwood timber mainly by machine methods.

List four aspects of making to consider when making a decision about which material would be best to use from a manufacturing point of view.

Products and quality

BBC GCSE Check and Test: Resistant Materials

Check the facts

Values in Design and Technology are covered in topic 27. They include technical values, moral values, cultural values and environmental values. A quality product will be designed to ensure that value issues are considered and, where possible, acted on.

In order to ensure quality in the application of values, a designer needs to consider the following points:

- **Technical values** – ensure that the manufacturing methods and materials used are accurate and result in a reliable product.

- **Moral values** – ensure that the product meets a defined need and does not cause offence to others.

- **Cultural values** – ensure that the product does not undermine the views of other cultures.

- **Environmental values** – ensure that the making, using and disposal of a product after use do not adversely affect the environment.

Test yourself

Consider one of the following products: mobile phone, personal stereo, electronic game.

List two aspects of each the values mentioned above which should be considered by the designer.

Products and quality

Check the facts

A designer needs to consider the following aspects of health and safety when designing:

- the safety of the finished product when it is used
- the safety of the finished product when disposed of after use
- the safety during the making of the product.

To ensure safety of the product when it is used, a designer needs to consider the following:

- will the product be strong enough to support the loads involved?
- are the materials suitable for the purpose? No adverse effects, toxic, harmful, and so on
- are all hazards sufficiently guarded? Electrical insulation, moving parts, folding components, and so on.

To ensure safety when a product is disposed of, a designer needs to consider the following:

- can the component parts and different materials be dismantled without harm?
- will dismantling result in the release of toxic or harmful substances?
- will recycling of materials, e.g. melting down, cause release of toxic or harmful substances?

To ensure safety during making, a designer needs to consider the following:

- will any of the materials specified cause harm to the maker?
- will any of the processes to be used cause harm to the maker?
- will any of finishing techniques used cause harm to the maker?

If any of the aspects listed above is likely to cause harm, then that aspect of the product will need re-designing.

Test yourself

List one safety point to be considered when making, using and disposing of the following products:

1 a folding push chair for a small child

2 a bicycle.

Health and safety

BBC GCSE Check and Test: Resistant Materials

Health and safety

Check the facts

All those involved in the making of products have a responsibility to use safe working techniques in order to avoid harm to themselves or to others.

Safety when making involves:

- safe storage and use of tools and equipment, including the use of machines
- safe storage and use of materials, chemicals, finishes and solvents
- safety in the use of flammable and toxic substances.

To ensure safety when making, use the following procedures:

- Store tools and equipment so that sharp edges and cutting blades are protected. Isolate power tools from the electrical supply.
- Operators should be fully trained in the use of tools and equipment.
- When using equipment, personal protective equipment should be used, including by other workers nearby, if necessary.
- Ensure all guards and other protective devices are in place at all times when the equipment is in use.
- Materials must be stored so that sharp edges and ends cannot cause harm.
- Wear gloves when handling materials with sharp edges.
- Store all chemicals, finishes and solvents correctly in accordance with the manufacturers' instructions. Some materials may need special storage away from other substances.
- When using toxic or flammable substances, use personal protective equipment. Take care to avoid excess contact with toxic substances and to turn off naked flames when flammable substances are used.

Test yourself

List one safety point to be considered in each of the following situations:

1 cutting thin sheet metal with tin snips

2 using a portable electric drill connected to a power socket

3 using a cellulose-based wood finish.

www.bbc.co.uk/revision

Check the facts

Risk assessment is the process of considering the hazards that could arise in a particular situation, and the risk of someone being hurt by the hazard.

A **hazard** is defined as anything that is likely to cause harm and/or damage.

The **risk** is defined as the chance that the hazard may cause harm and/or damage.

Risk assessment is defined as how likely it is that harm or damage will be caused.

When planning the making of a product, a designer may need to carry out risk assessments relating to materials, processes or finishes. Regulations and technical information should be consulted to identify the potential hazards. Ideally, the hazard should be eliminated totally. Where this is not possible, the hazard should be reduced by the use of protective equipment, such as guards on machines, extraction systems or personal protection equipment. If the hazard cannot be reduced to an acceptably safe level, the process should not be carried out.

Test yourself

Identify one risk involved when carrying out each of the following processes and then state a way in which that risk could be reduced.

1 Gluing acrylic using Tensol cement.

2 Using an electric soldering iron.

3 Using a wood-turning lathe.

Health and safety

BBC GCSE Check and Test: Resistant Materials

Check the facts

Health and safety

The following are provided in order to give personal safety to makers, both in industry and in schools and colleges:

- personal protection equipment – overalls, gloves, eye protection, ear protection, barrier creams

- guards on machines

- extraction systems for dust and toxic fumes.

All organisations have a responsibility to supply suitable protective equipment where it is required. Such equipment has to be kept in good condition. All workers, including those in schools and colleges, have a responsibility to use the equipment provided.

Personal safety has to be considered in the disposal of waste materials, including chemicals and solvents. Where necessary, chemicals should be neutralised by appropriate chemical processes. Some materials may need to be stored in special containers and collected by licensed waste disposal contractors.

Test yourself

List personal protection procedures needed when carrying out each of the following processes:

1 pouring molten aluminium into a sand mould

2 soldering an electrical circuit

3 using a drilling machine to drill acrylic sheet.

Check the facts

Health and safety in relation to environmental effects is concerned with the following points:

- chemicals that are used in the making or finishing of products

- chemicals that are used to make the product function, e.g. CFCs

- the disposal of products after use

- the recycling of materials and components.

When designing products, designers need to consider how adverse environmental effects can be avoided. This may mean the use of alternative processes, materials or chemicals. The use of alternatives may mean that some parts of the product need to be re-designed or an alternative manufacturing process needs to be used.

Current concerns about the environment mean that disposal of products after use has to be considered in the initial design. Methods of separating components and recycling materials have to be built into the design.

Test yourself

Consider one of the following products:

1 a bicycle

2 a printer for a computer.

List four things a designer would have to consider if materials and/or components used in one of these products were to be re-used.

Health and safety

BBC GCSE Check and Test: Resistant Materials

Usually designers produce ideas for products in response to market forces. Sometimes this is called **consumer pull**. Examples of market forces include:

- a demand from consumers for new or improved products

- a competing product is launched by another manufacturer

- a manufacturer wants to increase its share of the market.

Products may also be re-designed because of changes in materials or manufacturing methods. This is sometimes called **technology push** Technological changes may allow a manufacturer to make the product more cheaply, or more efficiently, thus reducing manufacturing costs.

Occasionally, a designer will design a new or improved product simply because they feel that it is needed or because a demand will be created by the very existence of the product, e.g. Sinclair ZX Spectrum personal computer, Dyson cyclone vacuum cleaner. Such a development may succeed or fail depending on the market.

Test yourself

List three aspects of mobile telephones that may have been developed to meet market demands.

Designer and consumer

A designer has a number of different functions to carry out and will often work in different ways, depending on the nature of the task in hand. A designer can function in the following roles:

Artistic and aesthetic role

This might be seen as the most creative aspect of the work of the designer, since such aspects as shape, form, colour, pattern and decoration will all need be considered.

Technical and/or functional role

In this role the designer is still being creative, but in a different way since he or she will be considering function, purpose, materials, systems, control, methods of joining, construction and finishing.

Economic and marketing, organisational and management role

A designer will also have to consider the economic and marketing aspects of the product, and these tasks will relate to the aesthetic and functional elements of the product. He or she may also consider the organisational and management issues involved in designing and making the product.

Test yourself

Investigate one of the following products:

1 a climbing frame

2 a wheelbarrow

3 a shopping trolley.

Identify aspects of the design that will show the different roles of the designer described above.

Designer and consumer

Designer and consumer

Check the facts

The relationship between the designer, the client and the user can vary, depending on the nature of the product and the quantity that is to be made.

In **one-off production**, the designer is frequently the maker as well. Even if this is not the case, the designer will almost always have a direct relationship with the client, who will usually also be the user of the product. Since one-off products are usually unique, it is essential that the designer is fully conversant with the needs of the client.

In **small batch production** the process of designing and making becomes more formalised, although the volume of the product and the number of people involved may still be quite small. The client may still be an individual, but could be a company that needs to design a new product using the services of a specialist design consultancy. In a batch production situation, the design team may have some contact with the user of the product but this will depend on the nature of the product and the user.

In **high volume production**, the processes of designing and making normally become much more formal and the making of changes can become slower. There is little or no contact between the designer and the user. The designer is therefore totally dependent on other people feeding back the view of users.

Test yourself

Suggest three ways in which the designer of a product that is made in large numbers can find out about the needs of the users.

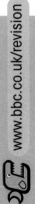

www.bbc.co.uk/revision

Check the facts

Consumer legislation and standards exist to protect the consumer from faulty or sub-standard goods and services. There is a wide range of legislation that can be enforced by trading standards officers who work for local councils. These include the **Consumer Protection Act**, the **Fair Trading Act** and the **Trade Descriptions Act**. This legislation allows consumers to be refunded if goods are found to be faulty or if products do not perform in the way claimed by the manufacturer.

Safety standards are an important guide to quality on which consumers can rely. In the UK, safety standards are set by the **British Standards Institute** (BSI). Manufacturers can use these standards to inform their specifications and to carry out their own testing. These standards can also be used by consumer organisations and trading standards officers as a guide when assessing a product. The European Community (EC) also sets safety standards known as **CE marking**. This legislation applies to all member states of the EU and requires manufacturers to display CE marking on the products.

The **ISO 9000 standards** apply to management systems, rather than to products. They suggest ways in which an organisation can be managed in order to provide a quality output. The ISO 9000 Series standards do not themselves specify the technology to be used for implementing quality control systems but suggest ways in which the company should be managed.

Test yourself

List three ways in which standards can assist in the production of high quality products.

Designer and consumer

BBC GCSE Check and Test: Resistant Materials

01 Writing a design brief
Design briefs need all the details on page 6.

Open brief
Lockable storage device for bicycles
Design a way to store bicycles (for travel to school) and prevent unauthorised use.
Storage of small objects
Design a way to display a collection of small objects.

Closed brief
Lockable storage device for bicycles
Design a bicycle rack, including a locking device to prevent the bicycle being removed.
Storage of small objects
Design a display case with clear plastic doors suitable to display a collection of seashells.

02 Writing a specification
Specifications should include all the relevant information from page 7.

Collection box for charity
The box must encourage people to want to donate money. It should have some sort of movement that is interesting/amusing; not be larger than 200 mm wide, 150 mm deep and 300 mm high; be made of wood, with moving parts from metal and plastics; must have a container for money. The moving parts will probably be two-dimensional, arranged on top of the box. Special requirements: the mechanism must be simple and not require maintenance. The movement will occur by the falling of a coin. Potential energy will be used. Anthropometrics and ergonomics will have to be considered in how the coin is placed and how the money is emptied. As the product is to raise money for charity, the cost of the product should not exceed £10. The product will be a prototype, but plans will be made for a batch of 50. There are no legal requirements, but the product must be safe and not cause offence. Materials used should come from sustainable sources where possible, and should be capable of being recycled after use.

Folding chair for exam use
The chair must support the weight of the largest person who might use it. It must fold up into the smallest possible space and be comfortable since people will use it for up to three hours at a time. The size of the chair will be determined by anthropometric data. The chair will be made from suitable sizes of wood, metal or plastics. The chair will need a seat and back support and suitable legs, the whole chair must fold flat. Special requirements: the chair must fold easily and simply, but must be firm in use. Anthropometics and ergonomics will be very important. The chair must be comfortable for all possible users.
The cost of the chair should not exceed £25. The product will be a prototype but plans will be made for a batch of 50. Legal requirements including any British Standards must be met. Materials used should come from sustainable sources where possible and should be capable of being recycled after use.

03 Developing initial ideas
1   2

04 Developing the chosen idea
1 Wood or wood-based materials. Solid timbers could be any of the timbers listed in topics 36 and 37. MDF and plywood could also be used if suitable finishes were applied.
2 The materials would be cut using a saw. If using solid timber, then the lengths could be cut using a cross cut saw or tenon saw. If cutting from sheet material, strips could be cut on a circular saw and then cut to length as above.
3 A jack plane or smoothing plane could be used to smooth the sawn edges. Final smoothing could be done with abrasive paper. In a simple product, lap joints would be used at the corners, and cross halving joints at the intersections of the parts. For a more complex piece of work dovetail joints could replace lap joints.

05 Using modelling to develop ideas

1 Welding rod if the product is made from metal tubes, balsa wood / strips of wood if the product is made mainly from wood.
2 Card or sheet plastic glued together.
3 Balsa wood if the product is made from wood, combination of balsa wood, metal rod and card if it is made from other materials.

06 Using testing to develop ideas

1 Find out the total mass of the objects to be put on each shelf. Test for bending when this mass is applied to the size of material to be used. Try a range of different materials.
2 Practise cutting a joint to see that the material cuts easily and does not crumble or split.
3 Apply a range of finishes to see which one works best on a range of materials.

07 Using testing to help decision-making processes

1 The angle should be within 1 degree of 90°.
2 The hole should be no less than 8 mm diameter and up to 0.3 mm larger.

08 How to plan the making of a product

Marking out sides and ends	15 mins
Cutting to length	10 mins
Marking joints	30 mins
Cutting lap joints	5 mins
Cutting housing joints	4–5 mins
Marking out partitions	5 mins
Cutting partitions	10 mins
Dry assembly and checking	15 mins
Adjustment of joints as required	20 mins
Gluing and assembly of sides	15 mins
Cleaning up of sides	15 mins
Approx. cutting of base to size	15 mins
Fitting of base to box	10 mins
Final cleaning up	15 mins
Varnish	10 mins

09 Wasting techniques – hand methods

1 Tenon saw for sides, 18 mm wide chisel and mallet to remove waste.
2 Tin snips for rough shape, then piercing saw and/or files.
3 Hand or flat file, second cut grade.

10 Wasting techniques – machine methods

1 Band or bench-mounted electric jig saw
2 Vertical milling machine.
3 Drilling machine.

11 Deforming techniques – two-dimensional shaping

12 Deforming techniques – three-dimensional shaping

Casings of electrical products, kitchen equipment, packaging, toys, and so on. Press moulding – see below.

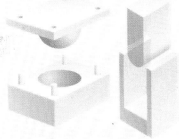

13 Fabrication techniques

1 Permanent methods cannot normally be taken apart.
   Temporary methods can be taken apart without damage to the product.
2 Permanent joining: wood – glued joint, nails; metal – welding, brazing, soldering, riveting; plastics – welding, adhesives.
   Temporary joining: wood – wood screws; metal – screwed fastenings, plastics – screwed fastenings.

14 Reforming techniques

Machine parts, bench vices, bases for sports equipment.

15 How to assemble and fit component parts of a product

Check that the joints fit correctly.
Check that the frames are at right angles.
Check that opposite frames are same.

16 Surfaces finishes

1 Gloss paint with suitable undercoat.

2 Suitable wood preservative.

3 lacquer

17 Using ICT

1 database or spreadsheet

2 spreadsheet, desktop publishing software, grahpics software, according to layoutof timeplan.

3 computer-controlled milling machine

18 Using ICT in industry

ICT could be used to assist in the making of almost any product made in industry: CNC punching machines to make metal parts out of steel sheet, CNC lathe to make turned parts (rods, screws, bolts, etc.) CNC milling machine to make appropriate parts, CNC router to made panelled doors and wooden shapes.

19 Using ICT for modelling

Ideas can be tried out before making the final product. Moving parts can be tested to see if they will hit other parts. The product can be viewed in possible environments where it will be used.

20 Industrial production methods

One off – used for products which are fairly unique, e.g hand made furniture, jewellery, toys, silverware, etc.

Batch production – used for small runs of a product, e.g set of chairs, small batch of toys, garden furniture, lawn mowers.

Mass production – almost all consumer products are made by mass production, e.g electrical equipment, cars, furniture, garden equipment, etc.

Continuous flow – small components, nuts, bolts, screws, gears, pulleys, electric motors, electronic components, etc.

21 Commercial manufacturing systems

Parts common to wall and floor fan: motor cover, electric motor, linkage to allow fan to rotate, fan blade, two part fan guard.

22 Packaging, marketing and advertising a product

1 Television, radio, newspapers, magazines, posters.

23 Quality control

Lengths/sizes of timber within 2 mm on length and width, 1 mm on thickness; Close fitting joints; Smooth surfaces, edges and corners rounded very slightly to remove sharp edges; Finish applied smoothly, no missed parts, no brush hairs in surface.

24 Using charts to plan the use of your time

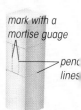

mark with a mortise guage

penc lines

Cutting the mortise

1 Mark out using pencil, sheet rule, try square and mortise guage.

2 Clamp wood to bench top. Cut mortise using mortise chisel and mallett.

3 Chisel down, lever out, waste wood. Go half way, then turn over.

4 Cross-section of roughly cut mortise

5 Smooth ends. Put chisel'? side to end and carefully re waste. Work from both side.

mark with mortise gauge

Cutting the tenon

1 Mark out using pencil sheet rule, marking knife try square, mortise guag

made with marking knife

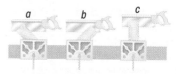

a   b   c

2 Put wood in vice to saw sides of tenon.

3 Cut the shoulder of the tenor using a tenor saw and bench hook.

4 Test fit the joint. Pare off waste if needed to obtain a good fit.

25 Testing and evaluating products
Use the points listed in the topic to check your answer.

26 Meeting the needs of the user
Use the points listed in the topic to check your answer.

27 Meeting value considerations
1 Technical – Is the table made well (close fitting joints, rough/sharp edges removed, good finish)? Moral – Is it the best use of materials, sustainable forests, appropriate cost? Where is it made (contribution to local economy)? Cultural – Why do we need such a table? Environmental – Source of the materials used: sustainable forest, energy used in manufacture and distribution? Is it recyclable?

2 Technical – Is the jewellery made well, e.g. parts fitted well, rough/sharp edges removed, good finish? Moral – Is it the best use of materials, appropriate cost? Where is it made? – contribution to local economy? Cultural – Why do we need such jewellery? Environmental – Sources of materials? Energy used in distribution and manufacture? Is it recyclable?

3 Technical – Is the unit made well, e.g. close fitting joints, rough/sharp edges removed, good finish? Moral – Is it the best use of materials, sustainable sources, appropriate cost? Where is it made? – contribution to local economy? Cultural – Why do we need such a product? Can we manage without it? Environmental – Materials source, sustainable sources, energy used in manufacture and distribution, recyclable.

28 Appropriate use of materials
Check against the points given in the topic.

29 Appropriate use of resources
Check against the points given in the topic.

30 Testing products and manufacturing systems (1)
Will the jig form the component to the correct angle? Will the jig be sufficiently robust in use? Will the plastic be held in place long enough so the material can cool?

31 Testing products and manufacturing systems (2)
The angle of the hole to the surface of the jig should be increased.

32 Classification of materials
1 Ferrous metals: Iron, mild steel, high carbon steel, silver steel, stainless steel. Non-ferrous metals: lAluminium, brass, copper, duralumin, lead, pewter, tin, zinc

2 Ash, beech, birch, cherry, chestnut, elm, iroko, mahogany, oak, teak.

3 ABS, cellulose acetate, nylon, acrylic, polypropylene, polystyrene, PVC.

33 Working properties of materials
1 Aluminium, copper, tin, lead
2 Ash, hickory
3 ABS, nylon, polypropylene

34 Ferrous metals and their uses
1 Mild steel, high carbon steel, silver steel, stainless steel.
2 Iron + carbon + 18% chromium + 8% nickel, + 8% magnesium.

35 Non-ferrous metals and their uses
1 Duralumin, brass, guilding metal
2 Aluminium + 4% copper + 1% manganese and some magnesium

36 Hardwood timbers and their uses
1 Iroko or teak
2 Oak

37 Softwood timbers and their uses
1 Scots pine
2 Hard, fairly strong, durable, straight grain.

38 Thermoplastics and their uses
1 Cellulose acetate
2 Tough, good resistance to chemicals, flexible, fairly soft, electrical insulator.

39 Thermoset plastics and their uses
1 Urea formaldehyde
2 Stiff, hard, brittle, good electrical insulator, resistant to chemicals

40 Wood
Common sizes for softwood timber:
25 x 25, 25 x 50, 25 x 75, 25 x 100, 50 x 50, 50 x 75.

41 Metals and plastics
Round mild steel 3 mm, 5 mm, 6 m, 8 m, 10 m, 12 m; flat mild steel 3 mm x 10 m, 3 mm x 20 m, 3 mm x 25 m; sheet steel 1 mm thick; sheet aluminium 1 m thick.

42 Standard components
1 Fixing two pieces of wood together, fixing metal/plastics to wood, fixing metal fittings to wood.
2 Machine screws, nuts and bolts.

43 Tools and processes for measuring, marking out and testing

1 Try square and pencil.
2 Centre punch and hammer.
3 Spring dividers

44 Precision measuring

1 11.9 mm
2 6.74 mm

45 Joining metal using rivets

Hammered rivets – to fix wooden handles of tools (kitchen knives, garden forks and spades, try squares) Pop rivets – for the casings of washing machines and tumble dryers, metal tool boxes, fixings in cars.

46 Joining metal using threaded fastenings

1 Self tapping screw.
2 Set screw, or machine screw, and nut.

47 Making screw threads

1 4.2 mm drill
2 Plug tap

48 Joining metal by soldering

1 Soft soldering using multi-core solder.
2 Brazing

49 Joining metal by welding

The metal is heated using a flame, which is a mixture of acetylene and oxygen. The metal melts and fuses together. A filler rod of the same type as that being welded is used to fill the joint if needed.

50 Reforming metal – casting

Make suitable pattern. Put pattern on board and moulding box round it. Fill with fine sand packing tightly. Make up top moulding box. Cut holes for runner, riser and pouring basin. Remove pattern and tidy mould. Melt metal and pour into mould. Remove casting when metal is cold and clean up.

51 The drilling machine

1 Twist drill
2 Flat bit, saw tooth bit.

52 The metal turning lathe and drilling in the lathe

Centre drill

53 The metal turning lathe – other turning processes

54 Heat treatment of metals

1 Medium carbon steel, high carbon steel. Tool steel and silver steel are other names used to describe high carbon steel.
2 Any cutting tool – knife blade, saw for wood or metal, wood chisel, cold chisel, centre punch, scriber.

55 Making the best use of standard components for metal

Each end is 690 mm long. Therefore the ends and three of the base pieces can be cut fom one 3 m length of metal.
690 + 690 + (3 x 450) = 2730 mm
The other three 450 mm lengths can be cut from another bar. This will leave 1650 mm of the second bar.

56 Types of construction using wood

Carcase body with frame of stool base.
Carcase body with plinth and framed door.

57 Joining wood using technical components

1 Knock down fittings.
2 Round head wood screw and washer.
3 Panel pins and glue.

58 Joining wood using joints

1 Housing joint.
2 Haunch mortice and tenon.
3 Bridle joint, Haunch mortice and tenon joint, dowel joint.

59 Deforming timber

The bowl is not suitable for laminating since the veneers cannot be shaped in three dimensions.

60 Making the best use of wood

All four of the legs can be cut from one 2 m length of 45 x 45 mm timber.
4 x 470 = 1880 mm
Cut one long rail and one short rail from one 2 m length of 70 x 28 mm timber.
950 + 750 = 1700 mm
Use another 2 m length for the other two rails.

61 Making the best use of standard components for wood

1 Butt hinges
2 Box lock

62 Shaping plastics by wasting techniques

1 Coping saw, abrasaw, bandsaw (teacher use only).
2 Files and then silicon carbide paper (sometimes called wet and dry paper).
3 Drilling machine – work held in machine vice; or hand drill and work held in bench vice.

63 Shaping plastics by fabrication techniques

The lap joint would be strongest because there is a larger surface area for gluing.

64 Shaping plastics by deforming techniques

1 Vacuum forming
2 Press forming and fabrication by gluing of other parts.

65 Shaping plastics by laminating techniques

Use barrier cream, protective gloves, eye protection. Work in well ventilated area. Teacher to mix catalyst and resin. Wear dust protection equipment when cleaning up cured resin.

66 Shaping plastics by reforming techniques – injection moulding

67 Shaping plastics by reforming techniques – extrusion

Curtain rails, electrical wire, tubes, gutters, water pipes, moulding to cover edges of kitchen and bathroom worktops.

68 Making the best use of plastics

69 Metals and ceramics

Shape memory alloy can be used to apply a pulling force in a straight line. Could be used for mechanical toys, testing of objects where a force must be applied, as part of an electronic lock.

70 Plastics and plastic reinforcement

Handles of tools and equipment where the part which is held must fit the hand.

71 Systems used in products

1 Mechanical system, electrical system
2 Cam and microswitch

72 System analysis

Input: wheels turn, moving connecting rod.
Process: connecting rod moves handle.
Output: figures move.

73 System design

The 90° movement would be achieved through the use of bevel gears. The driving gear should be twice the diameter of the driven gear. The reciprocating movement would be achieved through using the cam.

74 Types of motion

1 Rack and pinion
2 Screw thread
3 Crank and linkage

75 Changing force and speed in mechanical systems

1 Pulley wheels with crossed belt, or two gear wheels
2 Pulley and crossed belt. The driving pulley must be smaller than the driven pulley. OR worm and worm wheel.
3 Pulleys and belts. The driving pulley must be larger than the driven pulley.

76 Levers

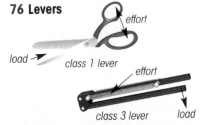

77 Using lever systems

78 Using pulley systems

79 Using gear systems

2 Bevel gears: one gear must be twice the diameter of the other.

80 Using systems thinking when making products

Look for examples listed in the topic.

81 Feedback – the drilling machine

12 mm hole in mild steel – medium speed
25 mm hole in oak – low speed
4 mm hole in acrylic – high speed

82 Feedback – the vacuum forming machine

Check for under cuts on mould, check for smooth mould, heat plastic to correct temperature, check vacuum chamber for leaks or misplaced mould or base.

83 Using systems thinking when designing

Accuracy	When check is needed
Medium Medium	1 – after cutting 2 – before cutting
Medium High	1 After cutting 2 Before starting to cut next part
High High	1 Before cutting 2 Before cutting

84 Using systems thinking when designing a product – example

Drill is cutting correctly (correct sound made by drill bit; waste material from drill correct). No excessive heat (feel material's temperature; check for smoke). Waste material prevents component fitting into jig correctly (visual check).

85 Designing jigs and fixtures

1 Have a stop that the material is pushed up to. Check no waste material is clogging the stop.
2 Have open corners so that waste can be brushed out. Have an open end to allow waste to be seen and removed.

86 Product design analysis

1 Base – mild steel, handle – mild steel, collecting tray – low density polythene.
2 Base – press forming, handle – press forming, collecting tray – vacuum forming or injection moulding.

87 Quality in designing and making

1 The materials can be shaped and formed easily by injection moulding. The materials can be self-coloured – no finish required. The materials are sufficiently strong for the job.
2 Does the fan blade turn without hitting the guard? Does the turning mechanism for the fan from side to side work correctly? Have the parts been moulded correctly? Do the electrical controls work as intended?

88 Ensuring quality in meeting the needs of the user

1 Passengers, cleaners, airport workers, buyer of equipment for the airport.
2 Passengers need a comfortable seat, perhaps for long periods of time; cleaners need a seat that is easy to keep clean and allows the surrounding floor to be kept clean; buyers of equipment need a seat which will last a long time and not look shabby; airport staff need a seat that passengers will want to use.

89 Ensuring quality in the use of materials and resources

Colour, ease of shaping, whether a finish is needed, or if it is self finishing, durability.

90 Ensuring quality in manufacturing

How easy it is to shape the material; the cost of the material; whether the maker has access to the equipment for cutting and shaping; how easy it is to join component parts; the type of finish required/necessary.